Snake Oil

GENUINE MARKETING
IN AN AGE OF CURE-ALLS

DAN RUSSELL

NEW YORK

LONDON • NASHVILLE • MELBOURNE • VANCOUVER

SNAKE OIL

Genuine Marketing in an Age of Cure-Alls

Published in New York, New York, by Morgan James Publishing. Morgan James is a trademark of Morgan James, LLC. www.MorganJamesPublishing.com

Proudly distributed by Ingram Publisher Services.

Morgan James BOGO™

A **FREE** ebook edition is available for you or a friend with the purchase of this print book.

CLEARLY SIGN YOUR NAME ABOVE

Instructions to claim your free ebook edition:
1. Visit MorganJamesBOGO.com
2. Sign your name CLEARLY in the space above
3. Complete the form and submit a photo of this entire page
4. You or your friend can download the ebook to your preferred device

ISBN 9781631958311 paperback
ISBN 9781631958328 ebook
Library of Congress Control Number: 2021950472

Cover Design by:
Ruth Cachares

Interior Design by:
Chris Treccani
www.3dogcreative.net

Morgan James is a proud partner of Habitat for Humanity Peninsula and Greater Williamsburg. Partners in building since 2006.

Get involved today! Visit MorganJamesPublishing.com/giving-back

for Melanie—to the ends of the Earth.

CONTENTS

INTRODUCTION

Mike Gets Ripped Off By An Ad Man

It always seems to start this way.

Fairfield Cycles, the bike shop that Mike started around six years ago, is experiencing its biggest sales slump to date. Revenue is down 70% from the same period last year.

Mike is sitting in front of his computer feeling stumped, so he pulls up Google and starts searching for a solution. A few minutes later, he finds himself watching a YouTube video that explains how Instagram Ads can help attract new customers to local businesses.

Excited by the possibilities, Mike starts posting on Facebook asking for referrals to people who can help him build an Instagram ad campaign. He gets dozens of responses from marketing consultants offering to help him. A little overwhelmed, yet committed to finding a solution, Mike books a few calls. Most of the calls end with a big price tag and a long-term commitment, but one call with a young marketer named Shilo seemed promising.

Shilo explains his approach to advertising, throwing out terms like "conversion rate" and "CPM." Mike could swear these were the same terms he heard in that video he watched. Shilo must know what he's doing. And his price point was within Mike's budget. So, Mike hires Shilo to build him an Instagram ad campaign.

There are two things that Mike isn't aware of at this point, even after hiring Shilo.

The first thing Mike doesn't know is that the cause of his sales problem isn't his lack of ads—it's his website. The site is outdated, not user-friendly, and doesn't have a way of converting visitors into leads. There's no form, his address and phone number aren't clickable, and the site isn't even mobile-friendly.

The second thing Mike doesn't know is that Shilo is what we call a MINO: a *Marketer In Name Only.*

(think of a minnow, the baby fish of the marketing industry)

Shilo, having recently completed an Instagram Ads training program, is naturally excited to have Mike as a client. This contract is the beginning of what Shilo hopes is a successful marketing agency. But that doesn't change the fact that Shilo is a MINO and has few marketing skills outside the realm of running Instagram Ads. That means when he's hired, Shilo is paying attention to only one thing: Instagram Ads. He has little experience with websites, so he doesn't pay any attention to how Mike's website is performing.

Mike, meanwhile, has never hired an Instagram ads expert, much less a marketer. He didn't take a class on hiring a marketer. He's a bike lover who started a business around something he loves. He doesn't know that MINOs exist.

Shilo begins building a beautiful Instagram ad campaign. Upon launch, the ads actually perform quite well. They receive a high click-through rate and send tons of people to Mike's website. Shilo is proud of his work and starts to tell his friends that his marketing agency is off to a great start.

But, as Mike will soon point out to Shilo, nobody is buying.

Mike's website is still performing badly, which means when people click on Shilo's ads, they leave the website a few seconds later. Mike may as well be lighting his cash on fire. But neither Mike nor Shilo know this.

So, after a few stressful weeks, Mike fires Shilo.

From Mike's perspective, Shilo was there to do one thing—make sales go up. Clearly, Shilo just wasn't cutting it. So Mike starts searching for a *new* solution while telling his entrepreneur friends that Instagram ads don't actually work that well.

Shilo, meanwhile, is blindsided by the firing. From his perspective, he was there to run Instagram ads—which he did. Successfully. So he takes a few screenshots of his ad campaign for his portfolio and continues trying to find clients who will hire him.

End scene.

Who *exactly* is at fault in this scenario?

Is it Shilo? Whose ignorance of a problem beyond the scope of his expertise led to the wasted time and money?

Or is it Mike, the business owner with a limited budget who assumed Shilo had marketing skills he never claimed to possess?

The answer is not a popular one—especially if you're a business owner:

The fault lies with Mike.

Let's simplify: if your car broke down on the side of the road, unless you're experienced in these matters, you wouldn't burst into the mechanic's shop and demand that they replace a specific part of your car. You don't know which part is broken.

And if you *did* do that, you can't hold the mechanic responsible for throwing his tools down, yelling *"you got it!"* and charging you for something you were sure you needed. It would take an experienced and honest mechanic to tell you to pump the brakes (pun intended) and figure out what the real problem is.

And yet, Mike did exactly that.

He burst into the mechanic's shop yelling *"give me some of those Instagram Ads!"* and Shilo was there to reply: *"you got it."*

It was Mike who spent money solving the wrong problem.

It was Mike who ultimately made the decision to hire Shilo.

Shilo wasn't experienced enough in the services industry to say, "pump the brakes," so a contract was signed and payment was made.

Okay—now for a little perspective.

Mike may have been at fault in this instance, but it wasn't his fault *that* it was his fault. Mike was the victim of authority bias. When we encounter an expert or figure of authority, we are more likely to respect their opinion and follow their instructions—that's authority bias. The power of this bias is compounded when someone is in a state of desperation, which is how Mike felt when he began reaching out for marketing help. He was out of his depth, and he knew it. So the first person he saw who fit into his budget and seemed able to fix the problem (in the way he defined it) became the expert in his eyes. Not just the expert on Instagram ads, but the *marketing* expert.

See the difference?

At that exact moment, Mike implicitly, unconsciously, and without communication placed the responsibility for his company's marketing on Shilo's shoulders. Shilo didn't have a clue. There was nobody at the wheel. Mike lost control of his business in a split second—and he paid for it. Not just metaphorically, either. He *actually* paid Shilo.

Stories like Mike's are becoming more common in the business world—including in the big business world of corporate contracts. MINOs, and even con artists, exist in those realms, too—the numbers just get bigger. The stories and lessons contained in this book will help you understand why stories like Mike's are so common, how to avoid falling into other common marketing traps of the 21st Century, and the strategies to build a marketing system that can help you strike a profit in the wild west of modern marketing.

If you're a business owner or marketing executive, this book will show you how to evaluate the marketers you hire and build a marketing operating system. With the right people and systems in place, your marketing will scale and support the growth of your business without ever being deemed a "cost center." The lessons that follow have, at the time of writing this, unlocked over $50 million in incremental annual sales for the businesses I've worked with through my marketing agency.

If you're a marketer, this book will show you the hard-won insights from hundreds of my conversion rate optimization campaigns. It will give you the right steps to reinforce your knowledge base of marketing and conversion principles. This includes neuromarketing conversion tactics, campaign planning processes, and critical audience segmentation techniques.

If you're a MINO and you're reading this book, I tip my hat to you and offer this: every time I take a step back to get into marketing "learning mode," I emerge a better marketer, even after all these years. Thank you for taking the time to invest in yourself through this book. Inside the pages that follow are the highly tested techniques and strategies that were behind those results. I invite you to use them to build your own portfolio of marketing successes.

What To Expect From This Book

Part One of this book will feel like you've fallen down a rabbit hole—**this is on purpose.** I want you to enter the same space an artist goes when starting a new painting. It's uncomfortable. It can seem chaotic at times. But once you emerge on the other side, you'll have something truly remarkable. Something you'll be able to call yours and yours alone. I'm going to share a little history, help you gain some perspective on what's actually important in marketing, and help give you a clear idea of *why* your customers will pay attention to you.

Part Two will show you how to plan and carry out a marketing campaign, how to leverage scientific marketing principles, and how to build a highly scalable marketing operating system. This is all technical knowledge, and I'll only be sharing it with you *after* I teach you about strategy in Part One. This is a backward approach to how most people learn marketing, and again, **this is on purpose.** I've given a lot of thought over the years to how my training programs are organized. If I taught you technical marketing skills before anything else, you'd end up putting those technical skills to use without a strategy.

One more thing: remember that a lot of other people are facing the same marketing challenges as you. There are tens of millions of businesses out there. If you feel like you're the only one who doesn't "get" something, the truth is that there are thousands, if not hundreds of thousands, if not *millions*, of people who are facing the same challenge. No matter the size or type of business you are in, whether you're a first-time entrepreneur or a seasoned executive, the lessons contained in this book are sure to give you a fresh and renewed perspective on the craft of marketing.

PART ONE

CLARK STANLEY, FAT SACKS, AND CHINESE ICY HOT

D espite its bad reputation all these years later, snake oil started as a legitimate product.

In the late 1800s, during the construction of the Transcontinental Railroad, thousands of Chinese immigrants came to the United States to fill the need for manual labor. They would spend their days swinging a hammer and, as you might expect, it took a toll on their bodies. Thankfully, they brought along all kinds of traditional Chinese treatments. One of those treatments was an ointment derived from the fat sack of a water snake commonly found in China.

This particular water snake had an exceptionally high level of Omega-3 fatty acids—higher than that of wild-caught salmon. When applied to the skin, it quickly brought down inflammation and reduced pain. Snake oil was basically like 19th-Century Icy Hot. And it *really worked.*

That is, until a man named Clark Stanley came along.

Stanley found out about the magical properties of this snake oil and wanted in on the action. He started to figure out ways to sell his own. The only problem was that Chinese water snakes weren't very common in the deserts of the western US. But you know what *were?*

Rattlesnakes.

Clark began concocting his own version of snake oil based on rattlesnake fat. It would have worked, too, if rattlesnake fat had an equally high concentration of Omega-3 fatty acids. But it didn't, which meant that *Clark Stanley's Snake Oil Liniment,* for lack of a better term, sucked.

That didn't stop old Clark, though. He started selling his fake ointment to as many people as he could find. As time passed, he realized he had to keep things fresh and innovative. Being a savvy marketer, he started adding ingredients like mineral oil, chili peppers, paint thinner, insecticide, and cooking grease.

Hardly the kind of treatment the Chinese had originally intended.

Before long, despite the real snake oil being an honest product, the popularized *Snake Oil* was diluted and twisted into a version that had no resemblance to the original. And since genuine snake oil was never widely produced by the Chinese, with no fancy labels or covered wagons to ship it across the country, snake oil began securing a reputation as a scam.

But the damage didn't stop there. Before long, other enterprising "doctors" came along with their own inventions, from *Dalby's Carminative* (originally an opiate given to babies) to *Dr. Pierce's Medicines* (which ended up containing high doses of morphine, cocaine, and opium). These fake cure-alls became known as "patent medicines," and they began selling faster than actual medicine.

The ingredients inside these patent medicines weren't regulated. Most of them were dangerous and are still illegal to this day. Patent medicines promised relief to people in pain, hair to those who were bald, and all kinds of other miracle cures. The result of all of them, however, was nothing but frustration, addiction, sickness, and even death.

The growth of these scams became such a crisis that, in 1906, the United States passed the Pure Food and Drug Act to curb the rampant sale of fake treatments. This act was a precursor to the creation of the FDA (Food and Drug Administration), which was established in 1916 and today strictly controls pharmaceutical testing and sales. Without this oversight and enforcement of health standards, the patent medicine crisis of the late 19th Century would have lasted much longer and led to even more problems.

The enforcement of standards helps industries grow at a rate that benefits the consumer, not the industry. Standards are a necessary element of any product or service that strives to be of high quality. Healthcare has standards. Financial services have standards. Food and transportation have standards. Almost every major industry has standards that protect the customers from businesses taking advantage of them or mistakes being made.

Even the marketing industry has standards. The FTC (Federal Trade Commission) is in place to protect consumers from illicit or misleading marketing. The CAN-SPAM act protects consumers from unwanted or abusive advertising practices. These and other organizations and acts of legislation are all productive components of the marketing industry—but there is a limit to their reach. The same benefits that the FTC offers to consumers like you and me are not extended to the Business-to-Business (B2B) Marketing industry which is filled with entrepreneurs and businesses who are trying to find marketing support from other companies, such as consultancies, apps, and agencies.

And this, my friend, is the recipe for history repeating itself. In the B2B marketing industry, innovation is so ripe, and regulation is so weak that hucksters have become indiscernible from professionals and the pressure to keep up with the "new" has caused businesses to make short-term decisions at their own peril. The true craft of marketing, like the original snake oil, is starting to become eclipsed by hype. Left unchecked, these forces will eventually land on your doorstep—if they haven't already.

A SPECIAL BREED

I'll never forget the look on peoples' faces at networking events when I said that I ran a marketing agency. Everything about their faces would change. Maybe you wouldn't notice it if you were in the conversation, but I did. I saw the subtle changes in their eyebrows, the angle of their lips, their forehead wrinkles, and their eyes darting around the room, looking for an exit. All were signs that I had immediately transformed into someone who couldn't be trusted.

Nor should I have been—after all, *I was in marketing.*

Professional marketers are among the least-trusted people in existence. According to a 2019 Gallup survey, the only professionals that are less trusted by consumers are car salespeople and members of Congress. When I was at those networking events, I felt like a snake oil salesman who accidentally wandered into a town he had already ripped off. Like the people I was talking to were afraid that at any point, I would pull out a contract, shove a pen in their hands, and yell *"Sign here! Or your business will PERISH!!"*

I knew this. The marketing industry has developed a habit of spitting out a special breed of scam artists in recent years. Not only did I know it, but other entrepreneurs knew it, and executives who hired guys like me knew it. For me, marketing's bad reputation was an occupational hazard, like an honest car mechanic trying to convince a customer that he's not trying to pull a fast one and the transmission *actually does* need to be replaced.

But things have been getting worse.

One of the reasons the marketing industry has achieved such a high concentration of scam artists is that it's moving so quickly—much like patent medicines in the 1800s. It's commonplace to hire a marketer whose specialty makes absolutely NO sense to you—because they're the only ones who have the time to stay on the cutting edge. When you are paying someone for skills that you can't verify, all inside an industry with little to no regulation, the chances are higher than ever that the bad apples will get away with their schemes.

So why isn't there regulation? If this is such a problem, wouldn't you think there would be governing institutions in place already?

Unfortunately, that's not the case. Regulation in the B2B marketing industry is impractical. Marketing moves and evolves too quickly.

Regulations are built on a static and unmoving standard of how an industry operates, and they serve to provide a rulebook for everyone to follow. This works great in industries like dentistry, medicine, and finance where there are strict rules around what you can and can't do. If you rip off a patient at your dental practice, you can lose your license. But there are no licenses in B2B marketing. There are no standardized exams, board certifications, or ethics committees. Which means if you rip someone off in the B2B marketing world, you can get away with it.

In B2B marketing, new platforms and strategies rise and fall on a weekly basis, which means it would take longer to set up regulations than it would for innovations to hit the market. If an industry innovates too fast for the laws to keep up, the laws have no point. And the marketing industry has been innovating like crazy—there's been a 52-times increase in marketing software platforms in the last ten years and it's not slowing down. No amount of regulation can keep that level of innovation under control. Even if the regulations *could* keep up, there's still no guarantee that they would be enforced.

Imagine a lawsuit brought by an e-commerce company against a malicious unskilled marketer who ripped them off. What would the lawsuit say? That the marketer couldn't achieve what was promised? There *are* no promises in marketing. It's like any other investment—there's a chance you'll lose.

Just for the sake of it, though, let's consider the e-commerce company's case. The prosecutor would have to demonstrate malicious intent, or at the very least, incompetence. Incompetence for a marketer would look something like selling an expensive marketing service without the knowledge of how to deliver the intended result. Two problems arise, though, at this point. First, it's no guarantee that the marketer and the client were aligned on the intended result at the outset of the relationship. Second, marketing skills are hard to verify, making it difficult to make a good hiring decision.

Remember the story of Mike and Shilo? Let's say Mike wanted to sue Shilo for incompetence. He would have to prove that Shilo made promises he couldn't keep. But Shilo did no such thing—he promised to carry out an Instagram ad campaign, and he succeeded. The numbers don't lie. It would be clear to the court that Mike hired the wrong person—not that Shilo ripped him off.

But, for the sake of our thought experiment here, let's say that Shilo had a twin brother named Riley, and Riley was the malicious marketer behind the e-commerce company's lawsuit. Riley took the same Instagram ads course as Shilo, but he started pounding his chest toward prospective clients, explaining that he was an expert in all things marketing. He presented the e-commerce company with a proposal that went way beyond the scope of Instagram ads, and in doing so began selling services that he wasn't able to provide.

If the e-commerce company wanted to get its money back and punish Riley, they'd have to demonstrate the same thing Mike would have had to demonstrate: incompetence. How do you think they would do that? By rifling through the textbooks in Riley's apartment? By opening up Riley's computer and seeing how many online courses he'd taken? The burden of proof would be on the e-commerce company—and the cost of acquiring the evidence to prove their case would, in all likelihood, be higher than just dropping the case. Without a method to determine whether Riley was innocent or guilty of being incompetent, the courts wouldn't be able to dole out a punishment or help the e-commerce company recoup their investment (and that's assuming Riley isn't broke and hasn't already spent the money, which is a long shot).

So the e-commerce company drops the case and moves on. Now its priority is to avoid encountering the same situation in the future, which means addressing the same challenge we've been circling this whole time: verifying the skills of new specialists whose technical skills can neither be explained nor verified by the person making the hire.

And the vicious cycle continues.

This is the same cycle that makes it easy for a college dropout to slap a marketing title on their LinkedIn profile, blend in with the rest of the professionals, and get hired. This is the challenge that businesses face every day—especially authority-biased entrepreneurs who have limited capital and are desperate for solutions.

Despite how bleak this sounds, there actually *is* a way to navigate this "wild west" of marketing. It starts with, first and foremost, getting clear on the types of characters you'll encounter on the road toward marketing success. Once you know them, you can avoid their traps and start investing your time and money in better ways.

THE WILD WEST OF MARKETING

Bethany runs a healthcare company in the Northeastern U.S. A few years ago, she was facing a significant marketing challenge. Bethany had a complex set of websites that needed to be merged into one "master" website. She had custom pages, blog posts, and all kinds of other content spread across each of her disconnected websites, and this digital chaos was starting to hurt the company.

It was a big project. So she began to look around for someone to help her migrate all of her content into one website. After interviewing a few agencies, she hired one that she felt was best suited for the project. The agency rep asked the right questions, knew the budget, and had a portfolio of success stories. They told Bethanie that the first step was to go through a trial period—an initial 30-day discovery process designed to create a tactical plan around merging the websites.

At least, that's what the sales rep promised.

Instead, a month later (and after $12,000 in investment), Bethany received a document outlining a *training* program focused on teaching her team how to use the new website. And it was over twice Bethany's budget.

She was stunned.

She didn't need a training program. She knew that, and her advisors agreed. Many thousands of dollars were invested into this agency—an agency that promised to create a plan upon which, until recently, Bethany was betting the future of her marketing strategy. Now it seemed it was all a waste.

8

When Bethany confronted her agency representative about the problem, he *admitted* that the plan wasn't what she requested.

What?!

It's like Bethany went to an Italian restaurant and got Mexican food. Usually, if that happened at a restaurant, you'd send the food back and request a refund. But, in this case, the restaurant didn't apologize and say they messed up (which would be chalked up to incompetence), but they said, *"yeah, it's Mexican food. Deal with it."* That's malpractice, ladies and gentlemen.

This is a normal Tuesday in the world of B2B Marketing.

In any other industry, Bethany would be able to report the agency to a regulating institution. Not in B2B Marketing, though. Bethany's options were to suck it up or go nuclear and sue the agency (which, in her case, would have been more expensive than the project itself).

When I interviewed Bethany about this story, I had a hunch about what had happened. I asked her a specific question: if it felt like she got a cookie-cutter proposal.

Fast-growing marketing agencies often standardize proposal templates and present them as custom-built plans. But, in reality, dozens or hundreds of other businesses have received the same proposal, each with a different paint job to make it *seem* custom.

Bethany said yes, it felt cookie-cutter. It seemed like they'd slightly tweaked the proposal to make it look like they had customized the project to her, but at the end of the day, it was an expensive Mexican meal that she didn't order.

Then Bethany said something interesting—she said it felt like she'd been lured into a trap by *Procrustes*.

I said, *"who?"*

She told me that Procrustes was a character from Greek mythology. He was a bandit who claimed to have a magical bed that could fit absolutely anyone, regardless of their height.

When Procrustes asked passersby to try laying in the bed to "see for themselves," he would *make* the bed fit them by chopping off their limbs or stretching their bodies to the point that it killed them.

A gross metaphor, for sure, but it carries truth—because it's what Bethany experienced. The agency was trying to fit Bethany's problem into their solution, and she felt the effects—in this case, betrayal and frustration.

There are three types of deceptive marketers that you'll come across in the wild west of marketing. Procrusteans are the first, but there are also Con Artists and MINOs (which we've briefly reviewed in the case of Mike and Shilo). I'll explore each form of deception in detail below.

The Procrusteans

Whether in the form of service or technology, marketing support is all based on helping a company reach leads and convert them into customers.

But every group of customers is different. Even within the same industry, even within the same niche, customer needs vary greatly. It is not uncommon to find two companies in the same industry and the same niche who don't compete with each other (something that authors Renée Mauborgne and W. Chan Kim call a *Blue Ocean*). An example of this outside of marketing would be shoes: some companies sell sneakers while others sell dress shoes. Same type of company, but different customer needs. B2B Marketing is no different. Some marketing companies sell sales enablement software while others sell social media services. Even inside a sub-niche like social media services, some customers need to build their audience while others need to run ads. Some customers are just starting out while others have an established audience. Some customers are in a highly regulated industry like healthcare while others are in unregulated industries like coaching. Having a social media agency, as a result, means that you have to build custom solutions for every client you onboard.

As a result, it becomes really, really hard to grow a marketing agency. Being in the services industry means that you are working directly with a company, getting on the phone with them, and helping them build a strategy that is specific to their customers and their products. That takes time and money.

As agencies grow, it becomes tougher to maintain this boutique, customized approach as client numbers start to increase. So they begin adding efficiencies by standardizing sales scripts and proposal templates. It's not long before these agencies fall into Procrustean behavior, where it becomes more efficient to stuff new clients into a mold that works best for *the agency*, not the customer. Procrustean marketers make the mistake of assuming that their standardized solution will work for everybody. This happens with consultants and consultancies as well.

In more cases than not, the clients sense what's happening—and then they get pissed. (Almost as pissed as they'd feel if their legs got chopped off just so they fit into Procrustes' bed.)

The consultants and agencies who do this are under the delusion that they are growing successfully. If Bethany's story was unique, I would say it was simply anecdotal. But this happens a lot. I've personally seen it happen over and over again. When you are a large agency or a successful consultant, economies of scale start to take hold and make it easier to grow. You have more resources for marketing and big sponsorships, which leads to more clients, more testimonials, and more case studies. It doesn't take much to start cutting corners to grow even faster.

When hiring an agency or freelancer to do work, it's essential to keep your eyes out for Procrustean tendencies—specifically in your initial conversation. Those tendencies usually take the form of leading questions or comments such as:

- Have you ever used [SOFTWARE PLATFORM]?
- You should check out [EXPENSIVE SOFTWARE YOU DON'T USE]
- Your marketing isn't working because you haven't tried our [SIGNATURE/PROPRIETARY METHOD]

These are all signs that they've prescribed a solution before you've explained the full problem. Now, there *are* situations where recommending platforms, partner companies, and signature processes is appropriate. But not in your initial conversations. When you ask someone on a first date, you're not going to tell them what restaurant you're going to—you're going to ask what type of food they like. Similarly, it's not appropriate for a consultant or agency to recommend a solution to a problem that they only partially understand. This is Procrustean behavior—fitting a problem to a solution rather than the reverse.

In Bethany's case, she hired a Procrustean marketing agency, which cost her time and money.

But it could have been worse.

There's another group of people out there who don't even waste time trying to deliver a solution. Their only focus is moving money from your bank account to theirs—so they can disappear without a trace.

The Con Artists

My friend Brandon owns a business in the food and beverage industry. About a year ago, he hired a marketing agency to help promote his services. It wasn't the first time Brandon was hiring a marketer, but he still didn't feel like a pro. This agency had fair prices and clearly knew more than Brandon did about marketing. So, naturally, he trusted that they were professionals.

It didn't take long for things to go sideways. Brandon started sensing their attention wasn't really "there" when they missed the first batch of deadlines. Brandon was only in his first month with this agency and was having serious second thoughts. But he thought this might just be how things go at the beginning of new agency relationships, so he hung in there.

Then things went from bad to worse.

One morning, Brandon received an email from the agency with an invoice for services he never agreed to. Things that Brandon didn't even understand. Line items with technical jargon filled with random fees and high hourly rates. He thought it was a mistake, so he reached out to them for an explanation, explicitly stating that they were not contractually authorized to charge his card for the invoice.

Welp… you can guess what happens next.

Brandon's phone dinged with an SMS alert from American Express. It was letting him know about the fat chunk of cash that the agency just charged from his card.

Fortunately for Brandon, this story ends well. Amex did the heavy lifting, and after a few back-and-forths with a lawyer and the merchant processor, he got his money back. But the legal fees had already stacked up and Brandon lost a bunch of time dealing with the situation.

The sad part is that Brandon got *lucky!* Imagine if he'd given his bank account information as part of an ACH transfer agreement with the agency. The money would be gone. He'd be screwed.

Situations like Brandon's occur on a daily basis in B2B Marketing. I could go on and on with stories like this. I am telling you—con artists are out there. They aren't *everywhere*, so don't go cancelling all of your credit cards and lose faith in marketers altogether. But they do *exist*. So, just like our parents and grandparents had to learn what a phishing scam looks like, businesses have to know how to spot a marketing scam.

There are three types of con artists. In psychology literature, there's something known as the *Dark Triad*, a collection of three mental traits—Machiavellianism, Narcissism, and Psychopathy—each of which enables someone to manipulate the world around them to get what they want. In other words, if someone is a Machiavellian, a Narcissist, or a Psychopath, the odds are higher (not guaranteed, but higher) that they're a con artist.

Psychopaths get a bad rap. It's a relatively common condition—about 1% of the population experiences psychopathy. That means when you're in a room of 100 people, statistically speaking, there's one psychopath present. But that doesn't mean they're going to viciously murder people. Being a "psycho," from a strictly clinical perspective, means that a person doesn't have the mental capacity to feel intense emotion or remorse for their actions. According to the U.S. National Library Of Medicine, "Psychopathy is a neuropsychiatric disorder marked by deficient emotional responses, lack of empathy, and poor behavioral controls."

Although there *is* a correlation with criminal behavior, that doesn't mean that person will become a criminal or a con artist.

Narcissism falls into the same category. According to Mayo Clinic, Narcissistic Personality Disorder is a "mental condition in which people have an inflated sense of their own importance, a deep need for excessive attention and admiration, troubled relationships, and a lack of empathy for others." Again, not necessarily criminal, and borderline advantageous if you want to, say, assume a high role in a government office.

The last of the three traits of the Dark Triad plays a larger role in the manifestation of con artistry than either of the other two traits.

Machiavellianism is a cocktail of exploitation, lying, manipulation, and feigned emotions designed to make someone do what you want them to do. As psychology researcher Richard Calhoon puts it, "A definition of the twentieth-century Machiavellian administrator is one who employs aggressive, manipulative, exploiting, and devious moves in order to achieve personal and organizational objectives."

This is the closest you'll get to a clinical definition of a con artist. When someone is talking about feeling "slimy" or "gross" after getting off a sales call, they've often encountered a Machiavellian sales rep.

There's a clinical test to measure *how* Machiavellian a person is—it's called the Mach IV test. It's used by psychologists all the time. Fifty years ago, psychology researchers Shelby Hunt and Lawrence Chonko released a research paper named *Marketing and Machiavellianism*. In it, they summarize the findings of a Mach IV test that they sent to 1,076 members of the American Marketing Association.

In the research, Hunt and Chonko go out of their way to note that "over 10% of all marketers in our sample scored in excess of 100 on the scale. Scores of this magnitude in the literature of Machiavellianism are generally considered to be very high."

Let me rephrase: **if you are in a room of ten marketers, chances are that one of them has a high likelihood of being a con artist.** Not guaranteed, but likely. And that was in the 80's before the internet made it easier to manipulate people.[1]

Knowing all of this, it is easy to understand why businesses keep getting ripped off by marketers. If the odds were that your car would violently explode 10% of the time you took it out to drive, we'd all still be riding horses.

So what's the problem that needs to be solved here? It's just all the con artists in the industry, right? We just need to find a way to *weed them out.* To get rid of them.

Well… not so fast.

Like Psychopathy and Narcissism, Machiavellianism might be an indicator of a propensity toward con artistry, and it is even straightforward enough to measure with a test, but that doesn't mean a person is a con artist. Re-read what I wrote in bold text above—one of them is *likely* to be a con artist. It's that dang *likelihood* that makes this issue so nuanced. Nobody knows who's a con artist at first glance, even with a Mach IV test. Which means we're back at square one. We need to figure out whether or not someone is actually out there to dupe someone else, not if they have the *ability* to do it. Unfortunately, modern technology hasn't caught up with reading peoples' minds yet, so we have to wait until con artists are caught in (or after) the act.

Not only is it nearly impossible to tell whether or not someone is a con artist before they perpetrate a fraud, but it's also a political headache to create the institutions necessary to catch them. Even then, those regulations probably

---

1   They continue in the report to outline the highest correlated variables in the experiment, all validated at a 99% level of statistical confidence. These variables ended up being gender, age, and marital status. Since the entire study was conducted using professional marketers, Hunt and Chonko were able to write this zinger of a headline:

"Marketers who are high in Machiavellianism have a tendency to be younger, female, and single."

Now, I know where your mind just went, so let me be abundantly clear: this does not mean that ALL young and single women in marketing are con artists. When it comes to research, sometimes you have to read between the lines. The researchers never mentioned this in their discussion, but if you were a young and single female in marketing in the 80's, you had to play hardball to keep your job, not to mention to keep your boss from making passes at you. This is an important thing to keep in mind—women may have had to display Machiavellian tendencies, even more so than their male colleagues—just in order to keep their jobs.

wouldn't even work. It took the SEC ten years to catch Bernie Madoff, and that was after ten years of *explicit tips mailed to their office* from a forensic accountant named Harry Markopolos.

If regulation doesn't work with the biggest financial fraudster of the modern age, how can we expect it to work in an industry where innovation moves faster than the financial sector, where data is more abundant than the financial sector, and where workers typically describe themselves as artists and have no universal requirements for employment, no industry-recognized certifications, and no method of verifying their skills?

No. Going after the con artists is not the answer. People have been getting ripped off since the dawn of bartering, and until we have some kind of Minority Report crime-predicting system, they'll continue to elude us until they perpetrate a fraud.

The con artist isn't going anywhere.

But things aren't so bleak—although the tactics used by Machiavellians are nuanced and powerful, there's a silver bullet that every business has at their disposal to protect themselves against hiring a con artist.

The reference check.

God, this one is so simple it's beautiful. If everyone just **called** and **spoke with** other entrepreneurs or executives who hired a marketer in the past, I probably wouldn't have to write half of this book. But not everybody does, which means the Clark Stanleys of the world can sneak into our businesses and wreak financial havoc.

Call your marketing candidates' references. If they don't have any, ask why. If they're not a MINO (which we'll review below), odds are they don't have any clients that would say good things about them. That's something you should know before handing them a contract!

The MINOs

This is the final reason why businesses keep getting ripped off.

Although it's difficult for businesses to know which marketers are good or bad, it's also important to realize there are also a lot of *marketers* who don't know whether *they* are good or bad.

Remember Mike and Shilo? Shilo was a MINO operating as an Instagram Ads expert. He had the expertise, for sure, but Mike's authority bias caused him to assume Shilo knew more than he did—leading to wasted time and money.

But MINOs aren't always innocent beginners like Shilo. Sometimes they're just delusional about their skills.

Some dude—let's name him Dude—can just wake up one day unhappy with his job. So Dude searches online for career options and stumbles across this ad in his Google results:

Start A Marketing Career—Fast Money
No Experience Required!!!

Dude is making minimum wage anyway—what's the harm in checking it out? So he clicks the ad and ends up watching a 60-minute webinar teaching him about some fancy new marketing platform, how it's going to change the business industry forever, and how newly minted experts are being paid the big bucks to help businesses leverage it. Then the webinar host pitches him on a $2,000 program to teach him all about this marketing platform. It even includes resources to help Dude start a consulting business to help *other* businesses use this fancy new platform.

So Dude thinks to himself, "*Yeah man, this sounds awesome! Entrepreneurship for LIFE!!*" and he maxes out his last credit card to buy the $2,000 program. A few hours later, he knows everything about this fancy new "earth-shattering" software, and more than that, he actually *believes* this tool is legitimately going to be the saving grace of businesses everywhere.

Keep in mind—Dude has never run a business, much less acquired the experience to know whether he is being taken for a ride. So, that night, Dude updates his LinkedIn profile to *Digital Marketing Consultant,* sets up a nice-looking website, and by the next morning, he's sending out messages to get leads on LinkedIn.

This happens—*literally*—all the time.

These kinds of "marketers" can put a company out of business very easily—especially when that company is small and has limited capital. Remember—there are next to no rules in the B2B Marketing industry. In B2B Marketing, businesses are on their own and left to their own devices. That means it's *not illegal* for a 22-year-old newbie marketer to drive your company off a cliff at 270 mph in the fancy new Bugatti they convinced you to invest in—foot on the gas, blindfolds on.

MINOs are the only category of deceptive marketers that I would actually recommend hiring—albeit in a very specific situation. I have some rules to hiring MINOs that will help avoid a situation as Mike and Shilo found themselves in.

Rule #1: Know when you're hiring a MINO

It's critical to know when you're hiring a specialist versus a generalist. In marketing, MINOs are all specialists. Shilo, for example, was an Instagram Ads specialist. There are MINOs for all kinds of marketing platforms and tactics. When you are conducting your interview, ask questions that cast a wide net across different modalities of marketing. For example, if you are hiring a marketing director, ask them if they have experience with graphic design, Facebook Ads, direct mail, and if they say yes, ask them to describe the project they worked on in detail. Even if you're not well-versed in any of those modalities, you'll know whether you're being misled.

If you get to the end of the interview and the person turns out to have a specialty in one particular marketing modality, such as TikTok, first tell them they're not qualified for the marketing director position, but also ask them if they'd be open to a more specialized role. Now you are speaking plainly and transparently about their skills—and they don't feel underqualified for a job that, quite frankly, they're underqualified for.

Rule #2: Measure the MINO based on their specialty

If Shilo had a job performance review from Mike, I would have given him a ten out of ten. Why? Because his ad campaign performed beautifully—it did what it was supposed to do. It sent people to the website. Oh—the website is terrible? That is NOT Shilo's problem. Shilo isn't a website expert. He operates in his little MINO bubble and builds his expertise.

If you are hiring a MINO, it's important that you keep them in their bubble. Treat them like an artist in their element. Evaluate them based on their performance, not on passively assumed realms of responsibility they blindly inherited upon joining your company. That's not fair to them and it wastes your time.

Rule #3: Encourage MINOs to learn and evolve

This one is my favorite rule because it leads to some of the most talented marketers out there. Given enough time, enough fair performance evaluation, and enough encouragement to try out new marketing modalities in a safe environment, MINOs can grow into sharks—and they will defend your brand, hunt down sales, and go to war for you.

Employer loyalty is a hard thing to come by these days. MINOs are, by their very nature, naive. That's not a bad thing, and the good ones *know* it. They'll tell you. Use that honesty and transparency as the basis for a multi-year relationship with them as their skills grow and evolve. You'll have the best kind of marketing team a company could possibly dream to have.

So where do we go from here? Now that we know about the Procrusteans, the Con Artists, and the MINOs, it can seem like there are fewer and fewer people out there who can help with your marketing. So, do we throw our hands up in the air and hope for the best?

No. And worry not—there is a light at the end of this tunnel. Now that you know the risky characters to keep a watch out for, we can focus on making the right marketing investments. To do that, let's rewind to a time when the chaos was kept to a minimum.

Sixty years should do it.

Back in the 1960s, marketing agencies were starting to become a new thing. They were scarce and highly sought-after. The original gangster of advertising, David Ogilvy, said this in his book *Ogilvy On Advertising:*

Introducing me at an Asian Advertising Congress in New Delhi the other day, the Vice-President and former Chief Justice of India said that I had 'mastered what Stephen Leacock called the art of arresting the human intelligence long enough to get money from it.' If there are still any natural-born liars in advertising, we are under control. Every advertisement we write is scrutinized by lawyers, by the National Association of Broadcasters, and other such bodies. The Better Business Bureau and the National Advertising Review Board (in Britain, the Advertising Standards Authority) review suspected violations of the various codes, and the Federal Trade Commission stands ready to prosecute us for deception.

Oh, how times have changed.

Today, those same institutions exist, but like the FTC, their primary purview is Consumer Marketing, not B2B Marketing. They deal with ads for things like Squatty Potty and Geico, not sales funnel strategy or webinar production. Malicious B2B marketers easily sneak under their radar. More to the point, that was sixty years ago—back when the B2B Marketing industry was, for all intents and purposes, nonexistent.

Ol' Man Ogilvy thought things were all right. He thought the industry was going to remain static and regulated, like finance or healthcare.

And maybe things *were* okay.

Maybe the industry *was* on track to remain static and easily regulated.

But history had other plans—and in 1989, a guy named Tim Berners-Lee, who worked at the European Organization for Nuclear Research (also known as CERN) invented something called the *hypertext transfer protocol* (HTTP).

And the internet was introduced to the human race.

KEEP YOUR HANDS AND FEET
INSIDE THE VEHICLE AT ALL TIMES

So here we were in the early 90's—boy bands, crop tops, windbreakers, and some newfangled thing-a-ma-bob called the internet. What some people don't remember (maybe you will) is that nobody thought the internet was going to "catch on." Techno-boobs and geeks alike had serious doubts as to its ability to reach mass appeal.

(Sidenote: Do yourself a favor and search "what is the internet, anyway?" on YouTube. Katie Couric and Bryant Gumbel have this hilarious back-and-forth about what the @ symbol means.)

All right—so this internet thing is catching on. A couple of universities get involved, websites start to become a thing, and before long, people start to wonder, *"hmm… I wonder if I can make money on this."*

And the roller coaster starts to drop.

The concept of E-commerce begins to emerge, but online payment systems are suffering from a trust issue. Nobody wants to put their credit card into an internet browser. Can't blame them—people only learned what an internet browser was about two seconds prior.

Then PayPal launches in (the year) 2000…

(remember when we said, "**the** year two thousand?" I used to think it sounded weird without the "the year" part, but now it sounds weird **with** it.)

Anyway, PayPal begins to revolutionize online spending[2] by serving as a middleman who can guarantee that the seller isn't a scammer and the buyer has the money. Trust in online payments begins to grow, but most consumers don't really notice yet. They're more concerned about whether Sony would ever make a Walkman that doesn't skip.

---

2   Technically, a company called Authorize.net was started first in 1994, but PayPal gained a larger mass appeal through its partnership with eBay and paved the way for more tech-friendly merchant platforms like Stripe.

While all of this is happening, Google is tinkering on something in its basement.

(Such a *nerd.*)

On October 23, 2000, they make a big announcement about this thing called *AdWords*. It was supposed to be this "revolutionary" self-serve ads platform.

Now, anyone, anywhere, at any time, can use AdWords to pay for advertisements that are shown to people based on what they're searching for on "the Google."

Keep in mind that by 2000, Google had grown at an astronomical rate; it was only two years old and was four years away from going public at a valuation of $23 billion. ALSO keep in mind that the total IPO (that's finance talk for a company going public) value in the U.S. for that year was $41 billion, which means Google accounted for over half of the total value of all companies that went public in 2014, including Salesforce, Air China, and Domino's Pizza. It was kind of a big deal.

Want to know why?

Because it had millions and millions and millions of people going to Google. com every single day searching for everything from "*how to install a kitchen cabinet*" to "*The Berlin Wall a decade later.*"

That's a lot of eyeballs. And that's a lot of people that *could* buy something.

Let me put it another way. You probably remember the Winter 2014 issue of Paper Magazine, right?

… No?

Well, you probably remember the cover. It's a picture of Kim Kardashian, butt-naked, with the words "BREAK THE INTERNET" on the cover. Sure, people talked about it, it became a meme, lots of blogs, yadda yadda.

People started to say that Kim Kardashian "broke" the internet.

But Kim Kardashian didn't break the internet.

It was done 14 years prior—when Google launched AdWords.

Here's why this is important:

AdWords was the first, ever, way to make money online at scale.

The operating words here are "*at scale.*"

That means that in 2000, if you had a product that made money, you could spend as much as you could raise—beg, borrow, and steal sort of thing, get a loan shark if you have to—until the cost of advertising rises higher than your cost of goods. Your customers were no longer limited to your zip code. Mom & Pop Donut Shop could now have instant global reach.

See, Google had one thing nobody else did—constant exposure to almost every human being using the internet.

Those millions of people were searching for solutions to their problems. AdWords gave those people a way to find the "best" solutions, and only at the cost of the businesses willing to pay for the sale. The customer paid nothing. So companies like eBay and Amazon and thousands of other companies started *pouring* money into advertisements on AdWords. Google became insanely rich, the advertisers became insanely rich, and the customers were happy they found solutions to their problems.

Meanwhile, PayPal's campaign for boosting consumer trust in e-commerce was starting to work. The general population had warmed up to the idea of pulling out their wallet in front of their computer, dusting off the number pad on the right side of their keyboard, and typing in their credit card number.

Enter stage left:

The internet marketer.

THE AGE OF CHAOS

A s the willingness to buy online grew, the incentive to capitalize on this grow-ing consumer demand grew as well. Early adopter businesses of the 90s as well as burgeoning entrepreneurs began to figure out new and creative ways to turn website traffic into money.

The formula was essentially this:

Step One: Write an ad on AdWords that promises to solve a problem that people are trying to solve with a Google search

Step Two: People click on your ad expecting to find a solution

Step Three: When they arrive on your website, you capture their attention long enough to get them to start reading. Then you convince them to pay you in exchange for solving their problem.

Step Four: Once you've convinced them to pay you, show them an order form and make it easy for them to buy.

This formula instantly generated billions of dollars for companies using AdWords.

Then, in 2005, Google stepped up their game, and AdWords launched something new called *Display Network*.

Display Network was a way for websites to make money by displaying Goo-gle ads to their visitors. That meant that if you had a high-traffic blog (of which there were many, including PostSecret, Lifehacker, and my personal favorite, car review site Jalopnik) you could start making money by displaying ads on your website. As a website received more traffic, more people saw the ads, and Google paid the website more money.

Google saw this as a way to increase its reach and make more money.

Bloggers, on the other hand, saw this as their ticket to early retirement. A way to write their content all day and get *paid* for it?! This was the new American dream.

All of a sudden, ads started appearing everywhere.

And I mean…

Everywhere.

Before long, the first internet millionaire was born.

Eventually, websites started to get smart and began thinking of other ways they could make money from the people visiting their website. They thought to themselves, *"If we can't display any more ads on our website, why not put ads ON TOP of other ads?"*

And just like that, the pop-up was born.

Before long, we had an internet full of thousands of pop-up windows that appeared as soon as we opened a website. I think if you pull anyone over the age of 30 out of a crowd today, they'd be able to go head-to-head against an 18-year-old shoot-em-up video game nerd just because they've had so much experience mastering the split-second reaction time needed to play the *close-the-pop-up-before-it-loads* game that everyone had to master back then.

As a result, people stopped being so gullible. Good thing, too, because things were just getting started. Get-rich-quick schemes had already begun to spread, touting work-from-home programs and promises of early retirement on a beach (for the low, low investment of just $4,999).

Sure, some people still fell for it, but the public was catching on. Pop-up click-through rates tanked, email open rates began to dip, and ad engagement started to fall.

In response, marketers got smarter. Neuro-linguistic programming became more mainstream as talented copywriters who could write persuasive content began flooding the market. Offline companies far and wide were on the hunt for the people who could help *them* get online and in on the action.

The internet gold rush was underway.

Meanwhile, another considerable force was quietly maturing in California.

The Shadow Lurking

Despite the quickly growing trend now known as "digital marketing," a more giant beast was forming. And it had been building in strength since 1999.

In 2001, this company quietly generated $5.4 million in revenue with a product that promised to revolutionize the productivity of companies' sales teams. By 2003, revenue had dialed up to a cool $100 million. This growth was tied to an innovative business model this company invented which is now known as **Software as a Service (SaaS).**

That company was called Salesforce, and it was the first of its kind.

Its founder, Marc Benioff, had a vision for a company that operated solely on the internet. It would collect payments on the internet, build its product on the internet, solve customer service requests on the internet, and most importantly, derive its valuation based on the number of people who paid a monthly fee.

At the time, the SaaS model was an earth-shattering concept. Until then, tech behemoths like Oracle and Microsoft (who sold the same kind of software as Salesforce) could only get their product to client businesses in one way. They'd write their software onto stacks of CD disks, fly their employees to client business offices, and install the software in person. The cost of employee salaries and travel (not to mention the CD disks) was incredibly high.

But with the introduction of SaaS, the now-adolescent internet was giving those big tech companies the ability to have their clients download complex software onto their computers remotely—and at a fraction of the time and cost of all those sales reps and CDs.

It wasn't like the SaaS business model was patented, so Microsoft and Oracle started using it immediately. Online versions of Microsoft Office and Oracle ERP followed in the next few years. Still, Salesforce had a considerable head start. To this day, Salesforce is the preeminent sales enablement platform in the world. Its reputation is so strong that more modern (and in some cases more functional) platforms *still* struggle to compete with the name recognition of Salesforce.

In 2003, with business booming at Salesforce, Marc Benioff met up for dinner with Steve Jobs. Steve told Marc that if Salesforce was really going to go all the way, it had to create what he called "application ecosystem." Marc thought long and hard about it, and eventually decided to start something called AppStore.com. He bought the domain name the next day.

It took three years to build Salesforce's App Store. It was the first of its kind—a marketplace of third-party applications that any user could plug into their existing Salesforce account, adding functionality in mere seconds with the click of a button and a charge to their credit card. It was a groundbreaking concept. Along the way, however, someone in the executive team drew the short straw and had to tell Marc that nobody liked the name. Fortunately, Marc was in a good mood that day and acquiesced to their coup—they renamed it from the App Store to the AppExchange. The launch was a huge success.

Two years later in 2008, Steve Jobs walks onto the keynote stage at Apple's headquarters in Cupertino to announce the creation of their own app ecosystem—coincidentally named the App Store.

(Side note—Marc, who was sitting in the audience, met Steve backstage after the presentation and gave him ownership of the AppStore.com domain. My guess is that Marc was sick and tired of hanging onto the domain and paying the $12 annual GoDaddy fee, but that's just me. Now it's *Steve's* problem.)

By this point, Apple has the user base and popularity to attract an even wider array of developers to fill its app store with all manner of apps, from games to business tools. Thousands upon thousands of other SaaS businesses begin to pop up, from Uber to Airbnb, fueling Silicon Valley's growth and the hunt for the next "unicorn" company[3].

This wave of investment and the massive reach of the app stores began incentivizing software developers worldwide to begin building software that solved every possible manner of inconvenience. It was just a matter of time before they set their sights on the marketing industry.

With the complexity of digital marketing increasing by the month, there was plenty of demand from businesses to solve very specific, very niche problems—from managing ads to tracking metrics. Building an app ended up being the easiest and most profitable method to solve those problems. Over the following years, marketing technology (now referred to as *martech*) became an industry niche unto itself. By 2011, 150 martech companies were building their own apps.

Then things began to go berserk.

Just a year later, in 2012, according to Scott Brinker, martech expert and editor of chiefmartec.com, the number of marketing technology companies had more than doubled to 350. By 2015, there were 2,000 martech companies in existence. And by the time 2018 rolled around, more than 7,000 martech platforms were offering some kind of app to businesses looking for marketing support.

The Micro-Niche

I don't use the word *exponentially* lightly. It has a precise mathematical definition, and I don't believe it's appropriate to be used as a form of exaggeration.

My wife, on the other hand, doesn't care. What's more, she knows it's one of my pet peeves (along with someone sneezing more than three times—no idea

---

3   A *unicorn* is a startup business that has achieved a valuation of at least a billion dollars. They're so named because such a valuation is rare in the highly risky startup investment world. Facebook, Airbnb, Google, SpaceX, Kajabi, and Udemy are some of the more popular unicorn companies.

why...), so naturally, she'll try to weave the word into a conversation that doesn't warrant its use, such as, *"It's exponentially hot today, isn't it?"*

Or "Babe, this sushi is exponentially better than the other place."

Or "Honey, don't you think XYZ band is exponentially better than ABC?"

Being a man of sound mind, emotionally steadfast in my handling of peeving moments, I ignore it.

Okay, that's a lie.

Most of the time, I'll go on a well-rehearsed tirade about the mathematical definition of exponential growth, how it plays a role in the world around us, how it differs from geometric growth, logarithmic growth, and arithmetic growth, and how it should never, ever be used as a means of blatant exaggeration. It takes about five minutes, and by that point, I've bored her enough to demonstrate the consequences of *peeving me.*

In this case, though, with the increase of martech companies between 2011 and now, the word "exponential" can be used (*appropriately,* mind you) to describe the industry's growth.

Normally, the exponential's job would now be complete, and it could go back to its sacred chamber wherefrom it could be called upon again for use by those more suited to its power than flagrant exaggerators...

...But in this case, the exponential needs to stick around.

Because the trend doesn't just stop there. With the creation of every new martech platform comes new ways to support businesses in using it—I'm talking about consultants, agencies, and trainings.

Let's say that a martech company launches a new analytics platform called Adooja. Adooja is a little complicated and requires some marketing expertise, so over the following few months, it begins to attract training programs, consultants, and agencies that have been built around Adooja. Their purpose is to help businesses leverage the full capabilities of Adooja. Before long, Adooja has given birth to a new martech sub-niche.

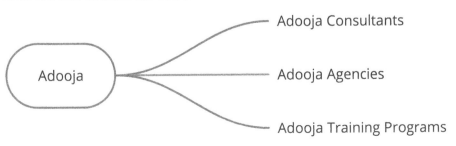

Let's be extremely conservative and say that Adooja has five competitors: Bopper, Credili, Disco, Elevant, and Fretter. If you were in the market for a marketing analytics platform, these are the options you'd find:

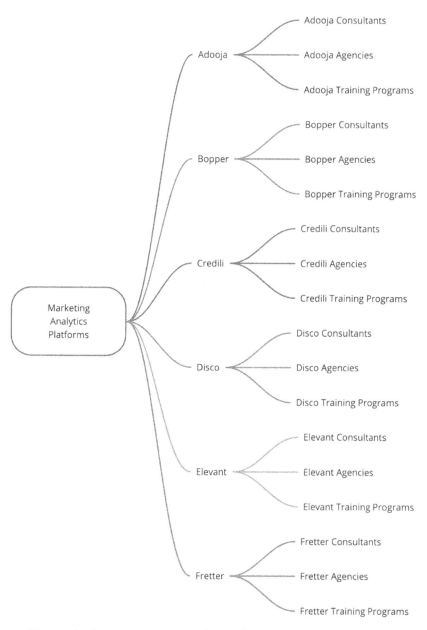

No wonder businesses are overwhelmed.

It only gets more intense when a disruptive platform hits the market, like a new social media app. As soon as that happens, new companies, consultants, and trainings rush into the market to fill the void of marketing support—in a niche that didn't *exist* before. It's like the universe suddenly expanded and now there are even *more* planets to explore.

This is why it feels so overwhelming when a new app like Tik Tok or Clubhouse hits the market. Not only do businesses and entrepreneurs feel that they have to learn *another* app, but they're overwhelmed with all of the gurus and agencies that start releasing support resources, each of which is *just a little different* from the last.

The longer a martech platform exists, the more confusing the choice between consultants, trainings, and agencies becomes. Take Facebook Ads, for example. It's one of the most prominent niches in the marketing technology space, right alongside Google Ads. There are apps that help you launch your ads, monitor your ad performance, and help you split test your headlines and videos. There are apps that use artificial intelligence to find the best-performing ad creative for your audience, apps that help you build your audiences, apps that write your headlines for you, and so on. And for every app that's launched, there's a consultant trained to use it and an agency building it into their packages.

Usually, this massive level of innovation wouldn't be a bad thing—a high volume of options means higher competition and more options for businesses. But we've gone way past the point where having more choices is a good thing.

I call this the *micro-niche* problem.

Need something to help you create your ads?

Need a platform to help you auto-schedule social media posts?

Need another one to edit and publish professional videos to your social platforms?

Need yet another to live stream to all of your social media feeds at once?

It's all out there. There are thousands of options. And these apps all do what they say they're going to do—nobody questions that. But there is a question that no entrepreneur or larger business seems to ask: *are these platforms adding value, or are they distracting us from the actual work?*

Let's look at an anecdotal example. Let's say my friend Eddie decides his marketing isn't working, and he needs to fix it. Within a minute of searching for inspiration on Google, ten marketing apps pop in front of his face on the search engine. They say things like:

You **could** write all of your sales copy yourself, or you could use our fill-in-the-blank copywriting software!

Tired of coming up with new ideas to post on Instagram? Use our artificial intelligence platform to develop the content your audience is looking for **in real-time!**

Why send emails to everyone at the same time when each subscriber opens their inbox at different times? Use **our platform** to send emails precisely when each person opens their inbox!

Suddenly, what could have been a productive creative session for Eddie turns into an expensive and time-wasting endeavor that only distracts him from thinking about the bigger problem. These apps are all piling up, each one seemingly more critical to use than the last, until the original purpose of Eddie's search is forgotten. He's now busy wondering whether his sales copy, his Instagram posts, or the timing of his emails are at the root of his problems—when, in reality, none of those options will help.

It's not Eddie's fault, either. Most of these platforms are built by intelligent marketers who understand their audience.

Hate copywriting? Just pay $300 a month, and our writers will do it for you.

Hate social media? Just pay $80 a month, and we'll post for you.

Hate ads? Just pay $50 a month, and our platform will manage it all.

These offers are everywhere, and it's not limited to software companies. Online courses, masterclasses, webinars, retreats, workshops, and challenges are all burying businesses alive with their offers, draining all possible time and attention away from the simple goal of building better marketing.

Runaway Innovation

In 2016, leading martech companies LeadPages and Infusionsoft released the *Small Business Marketing Trends Report.* They reveal that 48.5% of businesses in the study reported they had no idea whatsoever if their marketing efforts were effective. Even more to the point, 13.9% said they were *sure* that they were losing money on their marketing.

Despite the advanced tools at their disposal, businesses are having trouble managing the most fundamental task of marketing: ensuring that one dollar of marketing investment turns into more than a dollar in revenue.

So businesses are, for the most part, flying blind. And a lot of them are on their own. The report cites that 47% of small businesses handle marketing independently with no outside support. I don't know about you, but to me, that sounds like a recipe for loneliness, overwhelm, and a higher chance of messing up when you do end up reaching out for help.

In the six years since Infusionsoft and LeadPages released their report, a follow-up report hasn't been published.

In 2020, four years after the LeadPages/Infusionsoft report was published, email marketing company Mailchimp released its own report. *They* state that 7,040 marketing solutions were available to businesses in 2019 (twice the number of platforms on the market in 2016). Despite that increase, 31% of companies said that marketing was *still* their number one challenge.

What It All Leads To

Marketing has micro-niched down so far that businesses don't know how to fix their own problems anymore. They don't know where to start, and they've been trained to look anywhere but their own creative minds for a solution to any challenge they face. Think about the last time you had a marketing problem. Did you begin by sitting down with a blank piece of paper in front of you to think of a creative solution? Probably not. You probably did the same as the rest of us—searched for help on Google or in a Facebook group, at which point you get inundated with people saying, "*do this!*" or "*do that!*" or "*let's jump on a call!*"

Rarely seen is the lone consultant who says, "actually, I think what you're doing right now is the right strategy."

Because they don't make money that way. They have to close deals. This means keeping businesses, primarily entrepreneurs (the motivated early adopters with an urgent need), busy in an endless, expensive quest for the magic pill that will finally solve their problem.

Is this ringing a bell for you somewhere? If so, then the next question is: what problem are these businesses *trying to solve?*

Is the problem that they don't have enough time to do marketing?

If that were true, people wouldn't sign up for hours and hours of webinars. They wouldn't buy courses they never complete. They wouldn't schedule endless calls with consultants making promises to fix everything.

Time isn't the problem. When a problem is big enough, we *make* the time to find a solution.

Is the problem that businesses can't keep up with the micro-niches?

If *that* were true, the market would have corrected itself by now. Entrepreneurs and businesses would have slowed down in buying new micro-niche training and hiring new micro-niche consultants. Demand would dip, so supply would have to fall to maintain prices—or the prices drop. But that hasn't happened yet—prices are as high as ever, and the supply of new micro-niches is constant.

The **truth** is that businesses *can* keep up with the micro-niches, *and* they make time for marketing, but they maintain focus only long enough to get the euphoric rush of doing something new. Marketing technology is like crack to businesses, especially entrepreneurs. You may be in this group, sacrificing your productivity to stay on the cutting edge. And when the rush of the "new" wears off, these businesses and entrepreneurs, just like Mike did after firing Shilo, write off the micro-niche as a dud and move on to the next one. After this happens a few times, exhaustion sets in and they throw their hands into the air screaming, "*Nothing will ever just work for me!!*"

In short, most businesses are making time for the kind of marketing that interests them—not the kind of marketing that generates results.

And it's *exhausting*. As soon as you start to wrap your head around one platform, another one hits the market. As soon as you master Facebook Ads, Instagram Ads appear. Once you got into a nice email marketing rhythm, SMS became the new thing. Right when you thought your Snapchat profile was gaining traction, Tik Tok hit the market.

It's like playing whack-a-mole.

As of now, no certification program or college degree has developed a curriculum that can keep up with these micro-niches. I've been doing this for a decade. I've read the textbooks. I've gone through the training programs. I've received the certifications. I am *really* good at this stuff, and I can't keep up with it all. And even if you could, all your effort would be wasted after a year when everything's changed. Keeping up with it *all* is an uphill battle.

So, to recap:

1. The creation of micro-niches is at an all-time high level of intensity and complexity,
2. there's no way to standardize the education of cutting-edge micro-niches,
3. which means there's no reliable way to verify someone's marketing skills,
4. marketing charlatans and con artists aren't going anywhere,
5. the government isn't going to come to the rescue,

6. and the entrepreneur has little to no manner of defense.

So now you're probably feeling at a bit of a loss, right? Even more overwhelmed now than you were before? Good—you now understand the scope of the issue. This is serious. But, my friend, now that you understand the problem, we can finally start talking about **what to do.**

YOU CAN STOP WORRYING ABOUT WHAT'S NEW

Time for a perspective shift.

If you're building a house, you aren't going to care if your carpenter has the latest hammer design, right?

No, of course not. You're going to care that your stairs don't collapse.

Because of the micro-niche mayhem, businesses have become inundated with new tools left and right. This has slowly indoctrinated entrepreneurs and executives into a default belief that being on the "next big trend" is more important than understanding the principles that drive their marketing's success. They've become more worried about the tools than they are about the quality of the carpenter—and as a result, for most businesses, the stairs are creaking.

There's one type of question I get more than any other from business owners and marketers. It all boils down to the same fundamental question: *What should I do?*

This question comes in many forms—like, "What ad platform should I be using?" or, "Should I still be focused on blogging?" or, "Do you think I should start an Instagram profile?"

My answer is always the same: it doesn't matter as long as you know what to *say*.

This answer annoys almost everybody.

But I don't care. I've been doing this long enough to know that the marketing modality is much less important than the message being shared.

Let me explain further. Marketing operations can, in some respects, be boiled down to two things: what you **do** and what you **say.** The fancy new software

34

platforms and the cutting-edge training programs are the **tools**—the **micro-niches**—and they are *secondary* to the message they are carrying. Anybody can be a software expert and **do** things like building a CRM or a sales funnel. But the people who can figure out what to **say** in that CRM's email broadcasts or on that sales funnel's page are the people in charge of the company. These people are much rarer than those who can just **do** things. **Doing** is a commodity—something a MINO might specialize in—but **saying** is an art.

Why?

Because your message—what you **say**—is deeper than something that can be explained in a course. It's a message that you can *feel*. That resonates with people. It's a message that, when someone in your audience hears, sees, or reads it, their ears immediately perk up. They start paying closer attention because you've shared something that they simultaneously agree with *and* about which they feel curious to learn more. That's the seed of great marketing.

But you know what?

It's really hard to do.

You won't come up with a message that truly speaks to your customers while sitting at a conference. You won't find it in a training. Your consultant won't be able to tell you. The only place you can have someone outside your company come up with an idea like that is to pay a million-dollar-plus retainer to a huge marketing agency on Madison Avenue. They're the only ones who have the resources to sit down and do one thing that smaller agencies and most entrepreneurs have been passively trained to avoid doing:

Sitting down at a desk, in front of a blank piece of paper, and coming up with a Big Idea.

THE CAROUSEL AND THE BIG IDEA

If you're ever looking for an entertaining way to learn what Big Idea marketing looks like, watch the AMC show *Mad Men*.

Every season is full of stories about how the ad industry worked in the 60s and 70's. It's a fascinating roller coaster ride led by Don Draper (actor Jon Hamm) as we follow his string of affairs, his stolen identity, a general habit of self-sabotage, and his ever-surprising marketing genius.

There's one episode in particular that I'll never forget: the Season One finale. In it, you'll find a scene in which Don Draper is giving a marketing pitch to the executives of Kodak. His assignment was to find a way to sell their new slide projector nicknamed *The Wheel*.

The *Wheel* was supposed to be the big new "thing." But Kodak kept running into the same problem—customers already knew what a slide projector *does*. They knew that if they didn't come up with a new angle, their product launch would fail. They needed something more—something that would cause people to want *this* slide projector instead of an older model. Being the head of creative at his marketing agency, Don leads the meeting.

So he sits the two Kodak executives down as they ask a question:

"Have you figured out a way to make this work? We know it's hard because wheels aren't really seen as exciting technology."

Don smiles, turns off the lights, and slides into a monologue so smooth it made his hair jealous:

"Well, technology is a glittering lure. But there is the rare occasion when the public can be engaged on a level beyond flash—if they have a sentimental bond with the product.

My first job, I was in-house at a fur company with this old-pro copywriter—a Greek named Teddy.

Teddy told me the most important idea in advertising is "new."
It creates an itch.
You simply put your product in there as a kind of calamine lotion.
But he also talked about a deeper bond with the product...
Nostalgia.
It's delicate—but potent"

As he says those words, Don begins clicking the slide projector. To everyone's surprise, there aren't professional photos sanctioned by Kodak—nor are they photos from the agency.

He's clicking through his personal family album.

His kids on a swing set, him holding his ear over his wife's pregnant belly, their heads covered in confetti on their wedding day, and other candid personal moments. He continues:

"Teddy told me that in Greek, "nostalgia" literally means "the pain from an old wound." It's a twinge in your heart—far more powerful than memory alone.
This device isn't a spaceship.
It's a time machine.
It goes backwards... forwards... takes us to a place where we ache to go again.
It's not called The Wheel.
Dramatic pause...
It's called The Carousel.
Boom!
It lets us travel the way a child travels.
Round and around...
... and back home again...
... to a place where we know...
...we are loved."

As the lights turn up in the room and it's clear that Don has finished with his pitch, the two Kodak executives slowly turn in their chairs to look at him.

Their faces are in a state of shock.

They weren't expecting *that.*

They weren't expecting to *feel* something...

They just needed a cute angle to sell their slide projector. But instead, they got something deeper. Something intimate. It was, in many ways, a sacred moment.

When did businesses forget that marketing is supposed to make us *feel* something in order to be considered good?

That's the whole POINT!

When you "do" marketing, you're setting out with the primary goal of finding some combination of words and imagery that add up to create an idea in your customers' minds—the same idea that you have in your own mind.

Those ideas can be sad, funny, poignant, terrorizing, nostalgic, or anything else. But they have to *do* something to you. In the best of cases, those ideas can achieve a level of deep intimacy in the same way the Carousel pitch did.

These aren't ordinary ideas. They're not something that comes to you naturally. That's what makes them unique. That's why I call them **Big Ideas.** I know it's not an original term, but it gets the point across. Big Ideas strike a chord. Immediately. Like the opening line of a great fiction novel, they make you feel something profound and leave you wanting more.

Has a TV commercial ever brought tears to your eyes?

I remember watching an ad that made me start to tear up. God, it was a thing of beauty.

It followed a few athletes and their journeys to the 2016 Rio Olympic Games, but it wasn't just about the athletes. Interestingly, the ad was a series of childhood flashbacks that revealed something unique about each athlete's relationship with their mom. The scared phone calls from college, dealing with bullies, an elevator breaking down, being scared of airplane turbulence, and other moments of doubt—all with mom by their side giving words of love and support.

The climax of the ad was all of these characters performing huge acts of athleticism after they had finally made it to the Olympics—and winning the gold. Then, after they win, they each run to their moms in the audience, hug, and share a tender moment.

Now, by this point, people are *already* crying. Trust me—I've played this ad in front of a lot of people. Tears are flowing.

But the ad isn't over.

It fades to white, and the words slowly appear on the screen:

It takes someone strong
to make someone strong.
Then:
Thank you, Mom.
Awwww!!
Then—all of a sudden—the logos start fading in.
Tide.
Bounty.
Pampers.
Gillette.
Always.
Then a gentle female voice says:
"P&G. Proud sponsor of moms."
WHAT?!
That was a Procter & Gamble ad?!?
WOW!
They freakin' got me!!

Procter & Gamble makes household items! What do they think they're doing, making me all emotional just watching their commercial? I'm happy and sad and nostalgic and confused all at once. This is ridiculous—but I LOVE it!!

Great marketing *has* to do this kind of thing.

It **has** to grab you by the collar of your shirt, shake you around, and say to you—*this is real.* It has to take you by surprise. It has to be relatable. And it has to point back to the company in an authentic way. That's genuine.

That's what great ads do—it's why some people (like me) watch the Super Bowl just for the ads. You've got to be on your A-game when you're paying $5 million for a 30 second TV ad. So those ads are almost always home runs.

It usually takes an entire movie to lead up to a tearjerker moment. Romantic comedies are the most straightforward example. We sit watching for ninety minutes enjoying the emotional build-up, and then finally, at the climax, the kiss comes and we all go *awwww!*

That single emotional moment takes an hour and a half of careful, highly engineered storytelling to strike a chord.

Super Bowl ads can do it in thirty seconds.

Why?

Because the companies and agencies that designed that ad spent the vast majority of their time staring at a blank piece of paper, waiting until they came up with a concept that struck a chord.

They waited for the Big Idea.

They don't go with their first idea, which we're trained to do in workshops and courses and mastermind events. Your first idea will *always* suck. ALL of my first ideas suck. Never, ever go with your first idea. Your *fiftieth* idea will probably suck, too. The people writing Super Bowl ads get that. They're no different from you or me—they're just patient.

They don't go with their fiftieth idea. They keep going until the floor is littered with crumpled-up notebook paper. But when the real Big Idea ends up on that paper, they know it. The hair on the back of their neck stands up. Their nerves start to quiver. They have a different reaction to the Big Idea than they did to the seventy-nine other ideas crumpled up on the floor around them.

That's when they know it's ready to move forward.

Here are some Big Ideas from some companies you may recognize. When you read the words, you may remember an ad that you saw that reflected the Big Idea. That's how memorable these concepts can be.

AncestryDNA: We are all connected

Coca Cola: There's a Coke for you

Turkish Airlines: Widen your world

Proctor & Gamble: It takes someone strong to make someone strong

Guinness: Made of more

Mini Cooper: You do you

Apple: Be a rebel

You may read some of these and think, *"oh, those are just the taglines."* And you'd be right. But the premise of your thought is incorrect—the Big Idea isn't based on the tagline. *The tagline is based on the Big Idea.*

It drives the *entire* campaign. It drives the messaging of the company for *years*. That's why it's the **BIG** Idea!

When the person, or team, at a company comes up with a Big Idea, it's not just the words that make up the Big Idea. It's the feeling the words create. The stories that appear in our minds. That feeling and those stories cannot come into existence without going through the collective failure of the seventy-nine (or however many) other bad, sucky ideas scattered across the floor. That's where the

Big Idea gets its power. And that's why Big Ideas are so hard to come by. Because to come up with one, you have to fail.

Most businesses, especially entrepreneurs, have been taught to be impatient; to not wait for the Big Idea. To avoid the failure. In fact, most of us don't even know what a Big Idea is. We're used to going for the quick marketing "win" that lets us launch on time and impress our clients or bosses, but the quick win isn't the same as a Big Idea. Quick wins will fade. They won't sustain conversions. People will question them. They won't protect your brand. But Big Ideas are bulletproof. They can drive a company's marketing for years, if not decades. Think of Nike's *Just Do It*—that's a Big Idea that's lasted a long, long time. A guy named Dan Wieden came up with that phrase in 1988—I encourage you to look up the story. It's fascinating.

The path to a Big Idea is not in the direction of **doing** more. It's not based on the latest technology trend. You can't get to it with "quick win" thinking, and it's not going to pop into your head in the middle of the night. You have to put in the reps and work for it.

THERE ARE NO SHORTCUTS
TO A BIG IDEA

The Big Idea is the driving force behind a company's entire message, and that message directs everything from advertising to blog posts to social media videos to podcast episodes. A Big Idea is *big* enough to drive conversations across every platform you want to be on.

Big Ideas could sound abstract and lofty, like *"the Carousel isn't a spaceship, it's a time machine,"* and they could be simple, like *"Mom is a hero."* In either case, the Big Idea communicates a powerful message that inspires deep thought and curiosity. That message—and not the tools being used—is what causes a great ad, a great blog post, or a great video, to be remembered and shared with our friends.

While Big Ideas are powerful, they *can* be easily overlooked. They can elude our grasp and comprehension as marketers. It happens all the time. The thing that differentiates companies that can find their Big Ideas from those that can't is a willingness to sit in the painful, uncertain feeling of questioning the value of their products.

When was the last time you sat in front of a blank piece of paper and started writing down what problems you solve for your customers? Not what people say in reviews or testimonials, but what you believe is at the root of why they bought from you in the first place.

The blank piece of paper is my favorite metaphor for this exercise because nobody does it. You know, except the big Super Bowl ad agencies with the time and resources to sit down and *think*. Most entrepreneurs and executives are so *busy busy busy* chasing trends and **doing** things that we don't stop to think about what we're **saying** along the way.

Your Big Idea is the driving force behind your messaging. Without it, people aren't going to connect to your marketing. I don't care what you're selling—if your customers don't feel an emotional connection to your brand, they won't buy from you. I know people who *hate* certain brands, and if those brands were selling the freakin' cure for cancer, these people wouldn't buy it. Seriously. You might know some people like that. That's the power of having the right brand and having the right Big Idea to drive your brand's message.

If your marketing isn't working, it may be because your customers tried and failed to find a Big Idea behind your company. They saw your ad or your blog post or your Instagram photo, felt nothing, and moved on to your competitor's product where they felt a real human connection—and *then* they bought.

I can guarantee that if you sat down for two hours in front of a blank piece of paper and wrote down every possible Big Idea you could muster, it would be the most valuable two hours you've spent on your business since you started it. Later in this book, I'll provide a guided exercise to help you through this process.

Yes, it might feel painful.

Yes, it may lead to questions you don't like the answer to.

Yes, it might bring up some unwanted emotions.

It's uncomfortable. It's supposed to be. But if you want to make a boatload of money in your business and impact thousands or millions of lives, it's necessary.

The creative process doesn't start out as an exciting joyride. It begins as a tortured examination of the potential worth of whatever it is you are selling. So, if you're an entrepreneur just starting out, or you've had trouble selling your product or service, the hunt for your own Big Idea will inevitably contain the thought that your offer is worthless. Which is a big-time sucky feeling.

But if you want it all, you have to suck it up. Every idea you come up with is another step toward a better product and better messaging.

One last thing.

At this point, it may seem a lot less painful to just open up Facebook Ads and click the big blue *New Campaign* button. **Resist this temptation**, along with every other temptation to start **doing** marketing, until you reach the end of this book.

It's easy to just hand the reins over to Google or Facebook. To be led like cattle through a bunch of predetermined steps asking us simple questions like "what's your campaign objective?" Well, *sales conversions,* of course!

It feels *good*! I *know* it feels good.

It feels like we're making progress.

It feels like we're being guided by the hand by someone smarter and more well-informed of our own product than we are. It feels like we're building momentum—and it's not at all painful. In fact, it *feels like a game.*

Why would you want to stare at that blank page when you have all of those easy pre-loaded steps and all kinds of pretty apps and templates to guide you to success? That's the safe space. The safe, expensive, and paralyzing place called **doing** things without **saying** anything at all.

And yet, all the while, that blank piece of paper is waiting.

I know you're ready to start building. I can feel it. Stay strong and stay focused on the lessons you're learning. You're closer than you think.

PART TWO

Woohoo! Part two! I *told* you that you were closer than you thought! Alright, this part of the book requires a short introduction.

Over the years of running my own marketing agency, I designed a way for my clients to manage their own marketing without me. While this was a terrible business move, I knew I wasn't going to be running my agency forever—I was already feeling burnt out and knew the writing was on the wall.

I wanted to set my clients up for success. I developed a way for my clients to organize their marketing to work independently of any agency or consultant. I called it a *marketing operating system*. Similar to the operating system of a computer, a company's marketing operating system provided the structure needed to maintain profitability and stay focused on profit amidst the craziness of marketing trends and a revolving door of agencies and consultants.

That may seem like a big promise, so I'll explain why it works. Over the course of the years it took me to create this system, I became obsessed with the science of marketing. I studied behavioral economics, digital marketing economics, social psychology, copywriting techniques, conversion optimization principles, and all kinds of other curriculums in an effort to remove the guesswork from the marketing process. It began as a way for me to get better control over the results I was getting for my own clients—but it morphed into something that could be applied on a wider scale throughout a marketing department. What resulted has been crystallized in the pages that follow. If you learn these principles, you won't have to be at the mercy of micro-niches or rely on consultants and agencies to figure your problems out for you anymore.

The marketing operating system is responsible for unlocking over $50 million in revenue for the clients we served over the years, and that doesn't even include the entrepreneurs and teams I've trained since turning my focus to marketing education. It's been tested in over two dozen B2B and B2C industries (from industrial safety equipment to wine delivery), on high-ticket and low-ticket items, and on both products and services. It's responsible for 1,000%+ increases in performance on lead generation and 300% increases in sales, all with minimal effort and lightning-fast implementation (you can verify these results on our website). There is no other way to organize your marketing, no other process that has the scope and depth of implementation, and no more deeply battle-tested way to secure your marketing success than a marketing operating system.

This is it.

Let's begin.

THE AGE OF THE MARKETING SCIENTIST

> *"The scientist is motivated primarily by curiosity and a desire for truth."*
>
> **Irving Langmuir**

I was having coffee with a friend who, alongside his wife, runs a very successful business in the personal growth industry. He and I were chatting about a few candidates that he was in the process of interviewing for a marketing position. After chatting about it for a couple minutes, I asked him how the recruitment process had gone. He told me:

"In my initial round of interviews, I asked everyone the same question: 'If you could have access to only two numbers in order to run a marketing campaign, what would they be?' and the number of people who had no idea what to answer was staggering."

This is a huge red flag, and it highlights the most important skill gap in marketing experts. My friend was smart enough to ask the single most important question if you really want to judge someone's true understanding of marketing.

The two numbers my friend was referring to were **cost per acquisition** and **customer lifetime value**. Every business has those two numbers, regardless of business model, industry, or margin level. When you hire a good marketer, they find these two numbers, subtract the second from the first, and determine whether or not you're making money. The number one job of a marketer is to turn one dollar in marketing investment into more than a dollar of revenue. So those two numbers should be their primary concern.

Unfortunately, a good number of marketers don't know this. They've either been so entrenched in the art of their craft or so distracted by their chosen micro-niche that they don't know how to actually make money for their client or employer.

Working with someone that can't answer the "two most important numbers" question is extremely dangerous. Without the leadership of someone who can, that person will spin their wheels and drain your budget by building campaigns that will never generate a profit.

It's usually difficult to find a word that describes the person who knows how to focus on the two KPI's and the importance of doing so. We can't just call them "marketers" because that's what everyone calls themselves. Sometimes, you'll see titles like *Performance Marketer* or *Growth Hacker*, but those are arbitrary titles with little meaning, and even then, anyone can slap that title on their LinkedIn profile. For the purposes of this book, we'll use the term *Marketing Scientist* to describe someone who can see the whole picture and ask the big questions. They are more concerned with strategy than they are with tactics, similar to the carpenter measuring twice and cutting once, caring only that his blade is sharp and not if it's shiny and new.

The Marketing Scientist has what you need. You want to hire a Marketing Scientist and keep them around. You want to read a Marketing Scientist's report. Most importantly, you want to *be* a Marketing Scientist yourself in order to find the people who really know what they're doing.

Does this mean you need to become a pro at all things marketing? No.

It means you need to understand the fundamental driving forces of marketing. That's the defining trait of a real Marketing Scientist—the ability to instantly see a company through the lens of the two KPIs question. To ask the tough questions. To not get distracted by the shiny objects and the new tools. When you can do that, you make better decisions and avoid distracting micro-niches.

Do Not Be Alarmed

Two of the objections I hear when I start using the words "marketing science" are:

"I can't be a Marketing Scientist. I'm not good at math."

and...

"I don't want to be a cold, calculating person when I need to put together a marketing campaign. Marketing requires imagination and creativity."

Trust me, I get both of these points. But they're both based on false assumptions. People *assume* that marketing science requires complex math skills and strips you of your right to use your imagination. And it's not true. None of it.

To explain, I'd like to pull an example from history.

Carlo Rovelli is a theoretical physicist and the author of some of my favorite non-fiction books. He is simultaneously a beautiful writer and a brilliant thinker—and would probably make for a good example of imagination at work in science himself if it weren't for an even better example he shared in his book, *Reality Is Not What It Seems*. In this passage, he describes the role imagination played in the life and work of Albert Einstein:

"Einstein was no great mathematician. He struggled with math. He says this himself. In 1943, he replied in the following way to a nine-year-old child, Barbara, who wrote to him about her difficulties with the subject: 'Don't worry about experiencing difficulties with math, I can assure you that my own problems are even more serious!' It seems like a joke, but Einstein was not kidding. With mathematics, he needed help: he had it explained to him by patient fellow students and friends"

I hope you read that correctly. Einstein was terrible at math—most people don't know that. But this wasn't even the point that Carlo Rovelli was trying to make. He goes on to write:

"It was his intuition as a physicist that was prodigious…Einstein had a unique capacity to imagine how the world might be constructed, to "see" it in his mind. The equations, for him, came afterward; they were the language with which to make concrete his visions of reality. **For Einstein, the theory of general relativity is not a collection of equations: it is a mental image of the world arduously translated into equations**…. Einstein's imagination had no difficulty in intuiting the cosmic mollusk in which we are immersed, that can be squashed, stretched, and twisted—and that constitutes the spacetime around us. It is thanks to this visionary clarity that Einstein managed to be the first to write the theory."

The theory being referred to here is the General Theory of Relativity. I won't go into detail here, but suffice it to say that this theory was, and still is, considered to be the greatest scientific achievement in the history of the human race, alongside the work of Isaac Newton. And Einstein created this theory *solely* from his imagination. He wasn't a math genius—he was a *creative* genius. One could even make the argument that being terrible at math *allowed* Einstein the mental space to be as creative as he wanted to be.

So if you've been thinking that being a Marketing Scientist requires you to be good at math or throw away your sense of imagination, I'm disabusing you of that notion right now. If a great imagination and simple math skills were enough for Einstein, they'll do the job for you, too.

Math

"What, EXACTLY, are the types of calculations that you need to complete as a Marketing Scientist?"

If you can calculate a tip at a restaurant, you can become a Marketing Scientist.

Simply put, you need to multiply and divide.

And you can use a calculator.

Pretty much as easy as it gets. We'll get more into this in a couple chapters.

Imagination

"How, EXACTLY, does marketing science use imagination?"

Having a scientific perspective on marketing *frees you* to be more imaginative. It allows you to stop worrying about **how** things will get done (as Einstein's partners allowed him to stop worrying about the math) and opens you up to think about what you will **say** to the world.

The first place this happens is in the formation of your Big Idea, which we'll be getting to soon. Marketing science gives you a framework to put yourself into the shoes of your customers and see the world through their eyes while *knowing with certainty* that they are, in fact, the people you want to reach.

A bit later in this part of the book, we'll also explore another creative tool used by the Marketing Scientist, along with all scientists in history:

The experiment.

Experiments (or, as they're known in the marketing world, *split tests* or *A/B tests)* are where the Marketing Scientist can put imagination to work. In the same way Einstein used creative experiments to test his theories, you can use your own experiments to try out new, wild and creative ideas on how to get better results for your business. I'm even going to give you a guide on what ideas to pursue first—the same ideas behind the $50 million we unlocked for our agency clients.

Before we get to all of that, though, we have to cover the fundamentals. Without these, no amount of science and experimentation will help you. That's where a marketing operating system comes in—it collects and organizes all of these elements together in a way that makes sense and is manageable.

THE MARKETING
OPERATING SYSTEM

A marketing operating system, in its most basic form, is simply a machine you install into your business. An engine. And like any good engine, it can speed up and slow down; it can tell you when something needs attention, and it can run without you thinking about it all the time. It's built of many complex parts that work together seamlessly to provide a simple and highly scalable outcome. In the case of a marketing operating system, that outcome is sales.

If the purpose of marketing is to drive sales, the purpose of a marketing machine is to drive sales faster and faster with minimal additional work involved. I'm not talking about branding right now—that's one *part* of marketing that we're going to explore, but the whole kit and kaboodle are about making money. If you disagree with that, then you're probably not making any money.

You've *probably* heard the whole "make more money" promise before. It has a shiny-object ring to it, doesn't it? The idea that, if you just use this one tool or strategy or platform, all of your dreams will come true and money will rain down from the sky as you sip a cocktail on the beach.

Allow me to disabuse you of this notion right now.

Building a marketing operating system is not effortless. It won't solve all of your problems. It requires attention and creativity and a whole lot of patience. But if you learn how to build it and maintain its parts, it will have a lasting and valuable impact on your company for years to come.

That's the one thing that nothing else in the marketing support world can do. You can't say that about a social media platform or a SaaS software or a training program. Those things come and go, rise and fall with popularity, become obsolete, and can cost a lot of money over the long run. A marketing operating system is different. It's a business asset. It raises your company's valuation. It improves your ability to scale. It doesn't require a consultant or ongoing training of any kind. And when new trends arise or shiny object strategies enter the market, it provides firm, objective feedback on their legitimacy.

51

How It Works

In the most basic terms, a marketing operating system is organized into three parts: your **Customers,** your **Campaigns,** and your **Conversions.**

Your **Customers** are all the types of people—with all kinds of combinations of behaviors, beliefs, and backgrounds—that your product is designed to help.

Your **Campaigns** are a series of highly coordinated messages that your **Customers** see, whether that's on social media, billboards, subway ads, or TV commercials. They are what get your **Customers'** attention.

Your **Conversions** are a set of steps that make up your customer journey, all the way from an initial purchase to an ongoing subscription. They are designed to take your **Customers'** attention generated from your **Campaigns** and turn it into a sale (or, ideally, multiple sales).

Together, your Customers, Campaigns, and Conversions form the foundation of your marketing operating system. **There are no other parts to marketing.** You can draw your boundaries now. There is a limit to the marketing universe, and it is these three categories. I guarantee—if you manage these three areas well, your marketing will flourish. You don't have to venture outside their boundaries to be massively successful. Each of these three components plays a critical role in your customer acquisition process. They exist for specific reasons and none of them can be skipped—otherwise your customers won't buy from you. But, once they're managed, they can withstand anything you throw at them, whether it's a financial hurricane or a flood of new technology.

FINDING YOUR CUSTOMERS

You're probably familiar with the concept of a *target audience*—that's the group of people your company needs to reach to sell your stuff. Well, if you don't know who you want to sell to, everything else after that will fail. Without a clear understanding of your customers, you'll build products nobody wants and fail to react to important market shifts.

See, you can't just go after *everybody*. You'll waste too much time and spend too much money. A lot of people tend to think if they could just get a Super Bowl commercial, all of their problems would be solved. Just get in front of as *many* people as possible and *then* you'll hit your sales targets. And maybe you would—it's unlikely[4], but let's say you did make a bunch of sales. Even then, you'd be back to square one a month later facing the same problem. Exposure is never the issue; you can get in front of almost every person on planet Earth through social media and search engine advertising—but why would you want

---

4   It is unlikely for the average business to make a meaningful level of sales from a Super Bowl ad for a couple of reasons. First, if the business is too small, they will sell out and leave money on the table. Second, if the business is naive, they'll overcommit to get more money off the table, leading to a bad reputation. Third, and most important, Super Bowl ads are all consumer-oriented ads (yes, even Squarespace and GoDaddy), which means there need to be multiple brand impressions before a sale takes place. One Super Bowl ad doesn't have enough influence to make up for repeated brand impressions across multiple platforms. When I was living in downtown Denver, Colorado, there was a new cellular phone company that launched a marketing campaign. They had billboards, they plastered the sides of every bus, they were in the bus stops, the social media feeds of people living in Denver— they were *everywhere*. That's what is necessary to get people's attention—it's not about creating one moment of attention anymore. You can't build highly scalable sales projections on a customer base that is constantly learning who you are for the first time. It's about stacking multiple moments of attention on top of each other until the person *recognizes* that they've seen you before. Then you're cooking with gas. We'll get to memory tools later in this book when we talk about NeuroTactics. But a business who bets the farm on a Super Bowl ad will, inevitably, become (1) out of capacity, (2) overcommitted, or (3) limited by their weak branding.

to? Unless you're a religion or a dictator, your best option is focusing on a specific group of people. If you can control *which* people see you and which people *don't*, then instead of investing in a Super Bowl commercial, you'd invest in showing your commercial during a particular TV show that attracts people who are in your target audience.

But it's also not *enough* to know which TV shows your customers like. That cut mustard in 1966, but today, you need to do more. You need to know your customers better than they know *themselves*. More specifically, you need to understand the *problems* your customers are facing better than they can describe the problems to themselves.

In the marketing world, there are a lot of methods that help you identify who your customer is and what problems they are facing. There are persona templates, empathy maps, client avatars, and plenty of other fancy "proprietary" methods sold by expensive consultants who promise to paint your perfect customer in a beautiful flurry of words and numbers.

Honestly, you can make it as complicated as you want. But at the heart of all those methods are two basic market research foundations: demographics and psychographics.

Demographics are ways of describing your audience with raw data such as age, gender, location, and income. Think about the data that a census collects—those are demographics. Another way to think of demographics is how your audience looks from the outside.

Psychographics are ways of describing the behaviors and interests of your audience, such as buying habits, hobbies, and interests. This may sound more qualitative, but it isn't. Social media gives us all this data. Another way to think of psychographics is to consider how your audience looks from the *inside.*

Together, these two targeting mechanisms can help you find your customers. It doesn't take much to figure out who your product appeals to when you have this structure. Let's explore both in detail.

Critical note if you are thinking right now: I already know all of this. I know who my customers are…

If you think you can skip the next chapter and you've got it all figured out, then I suggest you throw away the rest of this book. Maybe you know who your audience is. Maybe you're even *right* about it (which is a long shot, given the depth of the next several chapters). But I guarantee you aren't revisiting this discussion on a regular basis. Going through the process in the next few chapters is **not—*I*** *repeat: NOT*—a one-time exercise. Your marketing operating system is going to *return* to this process on a regular basis. Your audience is not a static, unmoving object. It's made up of human beings. And human beings grow older. Their tastes change. Politics change. Culture changes. Technology changes. All sorts of stuff *constantly changes*. This is easy to forget when we enter the universe of business in which unattainably static objects reign: the evergreen funnel, passive income, and make-money-while-you-sleep promises that never come to fruition.

Furthermore, if you *think* you know who your audience is, *and* if there's just one element of the next few chapters that helps you identify a better way to "zone in" on your audience, then you're going to miss out. So, regardless of how much you know (or don't know) about your audience, get ready to roll up your sleeves, dig in your heels, and follow me into Willy Wonka's chocolate river of marketing marvels.

Customers vs. Audiences

There is a difference between Customers and Audiences. In the pages that follow, I'm going to be using the term *audience* to describe subsections of your Customers. We do this in marketing for a very specific reason: different customers buy your product for different reasons.

If I ran a local flower shop, I could describe my Customers with only very general terms: people who want flowers. That's not super helpful for marketing purposes. That leads to general and ineffective marketing content, like a headline that says, "Do you want flowers?"

Not very compelling.

Those who focus on Audiences, on the other hand, go deeper. They use demographics and psychographics to help identify the specific segments of their customer base which share certain traits. In the case of my flower shop, I would have an audience of husbands who have an upcoming anniversary, or college students in long-distance relationships, or couples with an upcoming wedding. All three of those audiences are comprised of people with a specific shared desire. As a result, you can leverage audiences for specific purposes, such as selling flowers at a bulk wedding discount or sending flowers to a girlfriend who lives far away.

As you move through the next two chapters, don't think about your audience as a single group. Think about your audience*s* (plural) and how you can mix and match different demographic and psychographic traits in a way that gives you a series of audiences, all of which fit under the umbrella of your total customer base.

DEMOGRAPHICS

Demographics are descriptions of people according to their outward appearance. We will be exploring the nine primary demographic traits in this chapter:

- Age
- Gender
- Income
- Location
- Language
- Parental Status
- Homeowner Status
- Education Level
- Job Title
- Life Events

Traditional marketing has relied on demographics to find the groups of people who are ideal to buy their products. Although they are the oldest way of finding your audience, they still play a crucial role in the audience identification process, so it is important to understand them. Let's get to it.

Age

In marketing, customer ages are categorized by generational groups. You've probably heard the names before, such as Baby Boomers and Gen X. These labels aren't just a way to describe how old someone is—they're designed to group people who share common beliefs that were shaped by shared social experiences such as a recession or a technological expansion. Although there are no universally-agreed-upon age ranges for each generation, markets tend to zone in on those ranges as time passes. There are currently four primary generational groups:

Baby Boomers (Born Approximately Between 1955-1964) are known to be independent and self-reliant. The *Telegraph* described it best by saying that Baby

Boomers include *"those born in the years after World War II, when there was—thanks to soldiers returning home—a significant spike in births, both in America and in Britain. These are the men and women who tuned in, got high, dropped out, dodged the draft, swung in the Sixties and became hippies in the Seventies. Some, like Bill Clinton, made it to the White House. Idealistic and uncynical, this was the generation that fought the cold war and smashed down the Berlin Wall."*

Baby Boomers buy a *lot* of stuff.

They are part of a large and aging generation. Their buying preferences are notoriously weighted toward in-person retail locations versus online purchases, reflecting their general discomfort or aversion to e-commerce. They have exceedingly high expectations of customer service representatives, which they will use as the basis of deciding whether or not to buy from a particular brand a second time.

Gen X (Born Approximately Between 1965-1980) grew up mostly without computers and were driven by a surge in entrepreneurial spirit. They grew up less career-oriented than their parents and thus switch careers, on average, about a half-dozen times over their lifetime. They also married later than their parents and often did so quickly, leading to a higher divorce rate than Baby Boomers. Gen X is often known as the MTV Generation, as they were coming of age as music videos, heavy metal and punk, and the show *Friends* were all bursting in popularity.

Gen X is the first of two generations who are at the height of buying power right now. If you are building a marketing strategy, a good place to start would be asking how you can position and sell your product to Gen X'ers to make the most of their buying habits.

Gen Y (*A.K.A. "Millennials"*) (Born Approximately Between 1981-1996) have been the most talked-about generation in the marketing industry in recent years, mostly due to the fact that Millennial spending power has begun to surge as their careers have begun to take off. Millennials are the first generation in history to grow up alongside technology. Most of them had internet access at a young age and are sophisticated when it comes to their experience and use of tech platforms and gadgets. Millennials are also nearly immune to traditional sales and marketing tactics, a trait that drove the rapid evolution of digital marketing in the late 2010's.

This group is also known as the *Peter Pan Generation,* a term coined by American sociologist Kathleen Shaputis, because of their tendency to put off major life milestones such as buying a house, choosing a career, getting married, and having kids. As Goldman Sachs published in their *Millennials: Coming Of Age* report:

"Millennials have come of age during a time of technological change, globalization, and economic disruption. That's given them a different set of behaviors and experiences than their parents. They have been slower to marry and move out on their own, and have shown different attitudes to ownership that have helped spawn what's being called a "sharing economy." They're also the first generation of digital natives, and their affinity for technology helps shape how they shop. They are used to instant access to price comparisons, product information, and peer reviews. Finally, they are dedicated to wellness, devoting time and money to exercising and eating right. Their active lifestyle influences trends in everything from food and drink to fashion."

If you are in marketing right now, Millennials are the big generation to focus on in addition to Gen X. Together, these groups make up a huge slice of the consumer buying pie. If you can position and sell your product to Millennials, you will end up with a successful company and a loyal fanbase.

Gen Z (Born Approximately Between 1997-2012) has never existed without computers and mobile devices. As a result, they treat technology as a social utility and believe it to be part of the very foundation of their lifestyle. They are known as *Technoholics* because of their reliance on technology for everything in their lives. Gen Z'ers are very focused on global issues, particularly global warming and human rights, and they make their purchasing decisions with a weight toward businesses that place these issues in their corporate agendas. Gen Z is made up of early adopters, making them the target for up-and-coming technologies such as virtual reality, artificial intelligence and self-driving cars.

There is also a "micro-generation" known as **Xennials** who were born between 1977 and 1985. They're known as the "Oregon Trail" generation (in reference to the classic video game—if you don't get the reference, it's okay, you're just not a Xennial). While Xennials differ in significant ways from Gen X (who didn't have technology in their youth) and Millennials (who hadn't yet graduated from college before the recession hit), they still have more of a pre-technology upbringing than Gen X and were more mature than Millennials when the 2008 financial crisis hit.

This means they already had jobs when the recession hit, *and* they had in-demand technical skills that Gen X didn't possess. This is a unique combination of experiences strong enough to differ significantly from either Gen X or Millennials, which is why Xennials are a micro-generation unto their own.

Because of their ability to group consumers by certain values, buying habits and shared experiences, generational groups are a convenient way of deciding what age range you should design your marketing around. For example, if the average age of your customers is 28, then you'd do well to expand your advertising to all Millennials, or ages 24 to 37. Generations are our first stop in deciding where our customers are. For now, decide which generation is going to be your target.

Do **NOT** choose more than one!

For the purposes of this exercise, we are going to get specific. You can come back later and create more audiences for yourself, but if you start out in this process with wishy-washy "my-product-is-for-everybody" thinking, you're going nowhere fast. Think of it this way: if I were to tell you I had a Baby Boomer, a Gen X'er, a Xennial, a Millennial, and a Gen Y'er lined up in a row and you had to sell to just one of them, which would you choose? You can't know anything else about them—just their generation. Whichever your answer is, that's the generation you'll start with when finding your customers.

The furthest I would go with overlapping generations in your messaging strategy is to include one "end" of a generation in addition to your core generation. For example, you can target Millennials and "low Gen X," which means you want to focus on the younger half of Gen X. This is helpful if you feel one side of a generation is still a good fit. But focusing on two separate generations is a bad idea—it's too broad and will land you in a pile of confusing content.

Gender

Gender is another demographic parameter you can use when finding your customers. Social platforms are able to differentiate males and females from one another, which makes it easier to target someone for a more specific message.

An extreme example of this would be if you were selling feminine products. The vast majority of consumers of tampons and pads are women; granted, plenty of loving husbands make last-minute trips to CVS to buy them, too—but for the most part, the ladies are the buyers. Same thing goes for male-oriented products like beard wax.

Most of the time, though, there's a pretty even mix of male/female orientation, even if the product is intended for a specific gender. Women often buy underwear for their husbands and men often buy flowers for their wives. Sure, guys can buy their own underwear and ladies can buy their own flowers, thank you very much, but it's not exclusive to one gender, even if the product is tailored to a particular gender (like men's underwear).

If you are in a specific-enough industry that requires gender exclusivity (such as tampons or beard wax), *and* you only want to speak to one generation and not the other, then choose a gender to target. Otherwise, build your content for both genders—unlike age and generational groupings, you don't *have* to choose one group over the other for the sake of targeting, unless you believe it's appropriate to do so. This is mostly due to the fact that consumption patterns are more uniform across different genders of the same generation than they are across different generations of the same gender. For example, a Millennial guy would have a similar willingness to buy from an Instagram ad as a Millennial female. Conversely, a Gen X female would have a lower willingness to buy from an Instagram ad than a Millennial female. See the difference? This is why I suggest that you choose a generational group at the same time that I suggest that you don't *have* to choose a gender.

Income

Income targeting is a *very slippery slope.* It's so easy to default to thinking that rich people are your cup of tea. Of *course* people with more discretionary income will have the money for your product. Guess what? Everyone else thinks that, too, and the price of advertising adjusts to compensate. As more businesses target advertisements to people in high income brackets, costs rise to advertise to those people.

Garrett J White is a guy who encountered a series of major struggles in his life, from marital issues to business collapse to being estranged from his kids. He embarked on a multi-year personal development journey to discover a way to organize his life to be in balance. Ten years later, he not only succeeded, but he also started a company called Wake Up Warrior to share his method with the world. To date, his business has helped over 50,000 married businessmen fathers gain more control over their lives by getting back in touch with their masculine power—what Garrett calls the Warrior's Way.

Notice how I described Garrett's business—specifically, who he works with. *Married. Businessmen. Fathers.* Right there, you can probably reverse-engineer two demographics. If the target customer is married with kids, he's most likely in Gen X, and the videos on the Wake Up Warrior website reflect that. If he's a businessman, he's a guy—obviously. But also notice the *business* part. This is an indicator of something else—not just occupation—but income. Wake Up Warrior charges thousands and thousands of dollars for their events—for good reason—and they want to make sure they are attracting high-end customers who own their own business.

Based on this, you may be thinking that Wake Up Warrior focuses on the top 1% (or so) of the population in terms of income—but you'd be wrong. For them to focus on the top 1% of income would also include targeting the top 0.1%, and the top 0.01%. They're not trying to sell to the Elon Musks of the world—sure, it would be great for Elon to come to one of their events, but there aren't enough Elons out there to make their business model work. Even though Wake Up Warrior is a premium offering, they still focus on a specific slice of the income pie.

Income is a critical demographic factor in understanding how to speak to your customers. Someone making three million dollars a year is going to respond very differently to an ad for a luxury suit than someone who's under the poverty line. More to the point, someone who has absolute control over how much they make (like a founder who limits their income for tax and liability reasons) has a different view of money than someone who is trading hours for dollars. You need to have a general sense of where your customers land on that spectrum. Once you do, you'll have a better sense of how to speak to them.

A good rule of thumb is that a high-ticket offer should constitute 5% or less of your customer's annual income. So, if I were selling an $8,000 program, I would focus on people making around $160,000 (that's 8,000 divided by 0.05). Ultra-high-ticket offers can go even higher, even over 100% in some cases, but I would use the 5% as a kind of guiding light. At the end of the day, you know your customers best. You understand what income levels are most appropriate for your offer and price point—but focus on the *slice,* not just a "this level and up" or "this level and down" approach to income demographics.

Also, to return to my point at the beginning of this section, don't go straight for the rich people. There are way more people in the world with normal incomes that have plenty of money to pay for your product. If you choose the top 5% or top 1% of income earners in the United States, you are excluding literally *billions* of people who could otherwise buy your product.

I'm not saying go for everybody—but don't go to the extremes. You should neither exclude nor be exclusive with high-income earners. Be realistic about the income level of the people you think are going to be right for your product.

A final tip is to focus on percentiles rather than dollar amounts. In this section, I've used dollar amounts to describe a customer's income level, but that was to make it easier to comprehend the concepts. Percentiles help you adjust for inflation. For example, instead of saying your product is focused on people earning between $40-70,000 per year, say your product is focused on the top 50% of income earners but not the top 10%. That way, your income targeting won't have to change every year.

Location

The next demographic trait we are going to review is location. This is probably the most straightforward parameter we will review, but there are still nuances to consider.

First off, location targeting has a multi-leveled hierarchy. The widest level of location targeting you can use is *everyone*, which includes every person on the planet. This is less than helpful, given that we are trying to specify both who is *right* for your product as well as who is *wrong* for it. You can't have a group of ideal leads without also having a group of less-than-ideal leads.

The best place to start with location targeting is your home country. There are a few reasons for this. First, it is a large enough group of people to target for exposure purposes. Second, your home country is a group of people with whom you share a common cultural bond. It would be difficult for me to write an ad for the Chinese population, for example, because I've never lived in China and I am not familiar with their traditions. Similarly, Chinese companies have to do a lot of research to translate their ads, both literally and culturally, to match the way that Americans read and interpret brand messages.

Considering these two points, it's easier to start by targeting your home country before expanding outside your nation's borders. Of course, there are exceptions on both extremes. On the one hand, if you are an American hosting an event in London, of course you'll want to build content for people living in the United Kingdom, which means using UK lingo. On the other hand, if you're a small business with an upcoming Labor Day sale, you'll want to be creating content for local radio stations instead of satellite radio, being sure to mention local landmarks that local listeners would recognize.

Choose your location—whether it is as wide as your country or as specific as your state or town. Whatever seems most appropriate—but the whole time, keep in mind how your messaging will be received by that population based on its cultural traditions, local slang, beliefs, and priorities.

Language

Of all the demographic traits we'll explore, Language is, by far, the simplest. Pretty much, if you speak English, write your content in English. If you speak Spanish, write your content in Spanish.

The only place where things get complicated in this category is (usually) with bilingual companies, particularly founders with personal brands. I've worked with a few bilingual companies over the years, and they always managed two separate social media brands to compensate for the fact that they had to include two languages in their marketing strategy. For example, one founder grew up speaking Portuguese and then, upon starting their business, realized that there was a huge market of English-speaking customers out there. As a result, they had one Spanish Instagram account and another English Instagram account. Having one account with two languages is a recipe for disaster.

If you happen to fall into this category and have two separate groups of prospects that speak two separate languages, my recommendation is to do exactly what this bilingual founder did and maintain two separate accounts across all of your platforms. This is the same strategy that multinational corporations use—for example, Nespresso has separate Twitter accounts for their global operations as well as Canada, Australia, UK & Ireland, and Japan. If you look at each of those accounts, you will notice that they are managed using different languages. The Japan account is, obviously, written in Japanese, and the Canadian account includes the use of the French language.

Bi- and multi-lingual strategies are relatively rare in the world of small businesses, but if you happen to have a bilingual or multilingual audience, it's a necessary step to take.

Parental Status

If someone is a parent, their priorities are vastly different from couples without kids. Their buying priorities, frequencies, travel plans, and all kinds of other elements of their lives are fundamentally affected by having kids, even if it is just one.

It is important to know whether your product is built specifically for parents or non-parents. Sometimes it doesn't matter, particularly in the B2B space, but if you are selling toys for toddlers, this demographic trait is going to be critical. Beyond the obvious example of selling toys, however, it is also a useful exercise to think about whether your product appeals *more* to parents than non-parents.

In one of our Marketing Scientist workshops, I had the pleasure of hosting a woman who was a co-founder of a company called *Ask Jenna*. They curated and crafted "going-out" plans for people who lived in Washington, D.C. The need was obvious—there are hugely diverse cultural, culinary, and social scenes in D.C., and it is hard for the average person to know about the best "hole-in-the-wall" restaurants or local events that they could explore. *Ask Jenna* did the work of scoping out those places, getting the best deals, and then giving people a pre-built plan for an evening, a date night, or a weekend excursion.

Now, with that in mind, do you think they should use the parent/non-parent demographic in their targeting?

You bet they should!

Imagine a husband and wife with two kids under the age of 4 at home. They probably don't get out much. In fact, they probably haven't been on a date in months. Don't you think having a marketing strategy built around that specific couple is a good idea?

Of course, there could also be a strategy for non-parents. And a strategy for single ladies. And another for single men. The point is that if you *know* you are talking to a parent with young kids, you can create better marketing that speaks to those people on a more personal level than if you just explained what your company does. And your sales will reflect that attention to detail.

Homeowner Status

This is an important demographic characteristic for two reasons. First, similar to the Parental Status demographic trait, people who own a home have different needs and problems than those who rent their home. For example, home service providers like plumbers and HVAC technicians aren't going to want to spend marketing dollars on renters—they would go straight for the landlord who pays the bill when a drain gets clogged or the A/C unit dies.

Second, and this is similar to the example I gave with *Ask Jenna*, the marketing concepts you create specifically for homeowners may be different than those who rent. Those who own their own home are more likely to spend time in one place for multiple years on end, whereas renters tend to move around every couple of years. This has important implications for local businesses reliant on repeat buyers such as country clubs and gyms, service providers like family accountants and attorneys (especially when licensed in a single state), and home improvement companies like Home Goods and Lowe's.

It is not required that you use Homeowner Status in your targeting but, as I said before, it is important that you *ask the question* of whether or not it plays a role in identifying your customers. You may discover a new and creative way to speak to homeowners, for example, in a way that generates more engagement than a less-targeted piece of content.

Education Level

Education level plays an important role in determining who your customers are. Knowing whether your customers are highly educated affects how you communicate with them. Someone with an MBA will respond differently to financial jargon than someone who has no training in business. Someone who only has their GED will likely listen more intently to content that contains blue-collar jargon. There are three approaches to finding the right Education Level for your audience: Top-Down, Bottom-Up, and Goldilocks.

Top-Down Approach

This approach is designed to reach everyone who has reached a specific level of education or higher. It excludes everyone else—for example, focusing on people with master's degrees and higher would exclude everyone who hasn't reached a master's level of education.

When using the Top-Down Approach, consider what education level your audience would need to have for them to (1) understand its value or (2) use it. If you are selling an advanced mechanical engineering certification, someone with a bachelor's degree (1) won't understand what you are offering and (2) will never use it. You must either move up a level to a master's degree or become more targeted in the *type* of degree you are targeting (once you get to the advertising stage, you can do this on LinkedIn by adding a *Field of Study* to your audience). We'll explore this more in the Job Title demographic section.

Bottom-Up Approach

This approach makes sense when you have a product that appeals to everyone *up to* a certain level of education. There are plenty of products and businesses that use the Bottom-Up Approach, from TV shows to restaurants. The key is to figure out how your product appeals *more* to those with lower levels of education than it does to those with higher levels.

This should *not* be confused with low income targeting; there are plenty of rich people who didn't go to college (and vice versa). Think about how you would speak to your audience *if the super-well-educated people had left the room.* How would your message change? Would you be more *you*? Would your brand message be heard more clearly?

A good example of the Bottom-Up Approach in action is theChive, a website that (according to its own description on Google) "brings you the funniest, the most outrageous, and the best photos and videos. You will never be bored at school or work again."

Sounds kind of juvenile, right?

Yep. And theChive is a *hugely* successful company. They turned what *The Verge* called Bro-Bait—basically viral videos—into a website that generates 20 million website visits and 100 million pageviews every month[5]. Then they launched The Chivery, a successful apparel line, and then a TV channel called Chive TV.

Altogether, these brands earn *$100 million per year* in revenue. The founder, John Resig, has an estimated net worth of $50 million.

And guess what education demographic theChive is focused on?

Students.

People who haven't graduated from college. They're sitting in their dorm rooms wondering what witty T-shirt they can buy next and sharing viral videos with their friends. This is the Bottom-Up Approach at work.

Goldilocks Approach

If you're selling a product that is tailor-made to a specific level of education, meaning not too high and not too low, you may need to *exclude* people on both extremes of the education spectrum. This is what I call the Goldilocks Approach.

One of our past clients was the world's most well-respected expert on handwriting analysis. He sold certifications to people who wanted to build a career as a forensic handwriting analyst, which he'd been doing for well over 20 years

---

5   The difference between these numbers is the number of repeat visits and pageviews that a single person engages in over the course of the month. That's 20 million people visiting, on average, 5 pages per month. In website terms, that's a home run.

(those are the people that courts bring in to determine whether someone's signature on a will, check, or letter is genuine).

When we worked together, I built a marketing system that would attract and convert new students to the school. We knew the marketing message was centered around the idea of starting a new and lucrative career, so we used education demographics to "zone in" on the segment of the population that had a high demand for that kind of thing.

We knew that someone who had an MBA was "out" since they would likely already have a high-paying job that suited their interests. On the other hand, we also knew that someone who only had a high-school education wouldn't have the level of expertise needed to complete the program and get hired as an analyst. So, we focused on the "Goldilocks" region of people with a bachelor's degree *but not* people whose highest level of education was a GED.

See how that works? Basically, we designed and targeted our marketing at people who had graduated from college (which automatically excluded people who didn't make it past a high school education). Then we *excluded* people who had a master's degree or higher. That was our Goldilocks zone.

Job Title

This is a powerful demographic trait. Knowing the job title(s) of the people in your audience is an easy and effective way to get laser-focused on the type of person you want to reach. The consequence of using this trait is that you will exclude a huge number of people who *don't* have the job titles you are focusing on. But then again, that's the entire point of marketing—finding and converting people in your niche. If you decide that your audience contains people who hold some version of Vice President in their title, you can plan your message in a way that will resonate with those people *specifically*.

A few years ago, my company was brought in to help a leadership coach launch a new sales funnel aimed at high-level female executives. Job titles became a front-and-center focus for our messaging strategy. It allowed us to focus on a segment of the population that we wouldn't have been able to define with Income or Education targeting alone. Once we knew the job titles of those people, we were able to craft more personal messaging that appeared across our sales pages, emails and ads in a way that appealed to women who held a specific level of seniority in their company.

We used the same strategy while working with an industrial safety equipment company. This company manufactured lockboxes that are installed outside of commercial buildings so the fire department can get in without breaking down doors. False alarms happen all the time in commercial buildings, but that doesn't stop the fire department from showing up and, if necessary, shattering windows and battering down doors.

Today, these lockboxes are legally mandated in most areas of the United States and this company has a well-known brand. So, it's safe to say they had a leg up from a marketing standpoint—but we still had to figure out how to reach the people in charge of buying the lockboxes. That meant we had to reach property managers, building owners and, in many cases, fire chiefs. We wouldn't have been able to craft messaging that resonated with each of those roles specifically (much less launch an ad campaign) without using the Job Title demographic. A fire chief will respond to a very different type of message than a property manager—and we knew that. Using specific job titles in our planning process gave us the clarity we needed to write personalized and compelling content—which ultimately led to a multi-million-dollar campaign.

Life Events

Life Events is a newer demographic trait aided by the growth of social media; thirty years ago, demographic targeting like this was not possible. This trait helps if your product or campaign is specific to a particular life event, such as a birthday or anniversary. Knowing that all the people in your audience are experiencing such an event will help you craft your message in a way that will resonate far more deeply than if you didn't know the event was happening. Facebook is the best platform for targeting people based on Life Event demographics.

Here are some examples of life events that Facebook tracks for its members:

- Anniversary within 30 days
- Anniversary within 31-60 days
- People who are away from their family
- People who are away from their hometown
- Upcoming birthday
- In a long-distance relationship
- New job
- New relationship
- Recently engaged

- Recently married
- Recently moved

These are all major events that open up a whole new line of communication for your audience. Someone who just moved into a new home has new desires and challenges they didn't have before. The same thing can be said for someone who is in a new relationship, just got married, has an upcoming anniversary, or is in a long-distance relationship.

Having the ability to specifically select your audience around this life event allows you to understand and relate to your audience in ways you would otherwise not be able to do. Think carefully about which of the life events I listed above could apply to your audience. You don't **have to** use this demographic trait, but if your campaign or product could benefit from speaking exclusively to a segment of the population experiencing a life event, then it is a good idea to start including this trait in your planning process.

PSYCHOGRAPHICS

Psychographics is the second method of identifying your customers. It is a relatively new addition to the marketing world now that we have social media platforms feeding us ever-more-detailed information about the people using their apps.

The Psychographics method is based on behavioral data points that aren't captured by demographics alone. Renowned marketing expert and author Seth Godin has the perfect explanation of the difference between demographics and psychographics, so I'll let him take the wheel for a second:

"There only used to be demographics. The only thing a marketer could pay attention to is *what kind of car do you drive? How old are you? What's your income?* You could buy all of those things from a mailing company.

But once the internet showed up, particularly Google, but mostly Facebook, we could say, 'this is for people who like that, this is for people who dream of that, this is for people who believe this.'

Those are psychographics.

It doesn't matter what your skin color is, it doesn't matter what your income is—it's what's your narrative inside… What we need to understand is in every zip code, there are people of almost every psychographic perception. What we must do as brand marketers is say, *'it's for you—and it's not for you. And I didn't separate you because of who your parents were, I separated you for what you believe and what you dream of.'*"

In a nutshell, if demographics describes what a person looks like from the outside, psychographics describes what they look like on the inside. All the soft stuff. Before social media, none of that could be measured unless you spoke to each person individually. Now, with the data provided by social media platforms, we can write marketing content for people who are avid online shoppers, those who skew toward liberal politics, and those who like gardening, vegan food, Oprah, or Whole Foods Market. You couldn't do that twenty years ago.

A Double-Edged Sword

The breadth of psychographics is a blessing and a curse. While psychographics offers us a virtually infinite number of ways to *find* people, they also introduce the problem of how to *organize* it all. Businesses often get stuck at this part when setting up an ad campaign. The question is always the same: *How do I create my audience?*

First things first. If you are in the process of designing an ad campaign and you don't already know your audience, you're already behind. This is what is happening when an executive or entrepreneur says, *"I'm smart enough about marketing to be dangerous."*

Right you are.

So, let's take a deeper look at how we can organize psychographics in a way that is easier to understand than just looking at all the options at once. There are three psychographic traits that you can use to keep it all straight. You can think of them as psychographic categories. They are:

- Behaviors
- Interests
- Connections

These three traits are based on how Facebook and Google organize their own psychographic targeting. Since social media gave birth to psychographic data, it makes sense to use their categories in our own planning. In a moment, we'll take a closer look at each of these three traits, but first it's important that you understand how this data is collected. It all centers around something called a *cookie.*

Cookies

Web cookies, unlike their delicious snacking counterpart, are pieces of code placed on your web browser. They serve a critical role in ad platforms' ability to track your behaviors online, and companies combine this tracking data with what they already know about you. Let's take a look at a quick example of a behavior attribute known as being an *early adopter.*

Early adopters are people who will buy a new gadget, toy, or software as soon as it comes out. They are the ones who sit in line to buy the newest iPhone or the latest VR headset. They have the discretionary funds to purchase these items and they do so willingly—even excitedly—in order to stay on the cutting edge.

Early adopters are a hugely valuable customer segment. If a tech company knows someone is an early adopter, they'll pay a premium to get their ad in front of that person. The problem is *figuring out* whether someone is an early adopter or just your average everyday techno-boob.

It is one thing if someone *says* they are an early adopter. They could be lying in order to fit in, or they may be delusional about what an early adopter actually is. Ask any psychologist if human beings are good at predicting their future behavior and you will get a resounding *NO!* every single time. We, as human beings, are ridiculously bad at understanding why we make the decisions that we do. This makes it impossible to objectively decide whether we would buy one product or another. This is the age-old flaw of focus groups; the number of people who *say* they would buy a product is always much larger than the number of people who actually do it.

So, to circumvent this challenge, companies *watch* what people do. In other words, they look at what you have done in the past to predict what you will do in the future. This is what a cookie does.

When you visit a website to buy something, like a new pair of shoes, and that site has a Facebook or Google tracking code to measure the return on the shoe company's advertising, your internet browser is loaded with the previously described *cookie.*

The cookie is a piece of code that's saved on your browser, and it follows you across the internet. Every time you visit a website with a tracking code (which is pretty much all of them), that cookie *talks to the website* and exchanges information like your Facebook and Google account IDs[6]. With that information in hand, that website *talks* to companies like Facebook to tell them what you are doing on their website. Facebook will then know that you visited that website— along with everything you did on that website. If you clear your browser cookies and then visit that site, you still get the cookie, and the next time you log into Facebook, your profile is updated with that cookie's data.

This allows websites like Amazon, Facebook and Google to customize your experience with their website and products in a way that is tailored to your interests, behaviors, connections, and life events.

Can it go too far? Absolutely.

This is one of the privacy arguments raging in Washington right now. A few years ago, a writer named Charles Duhigg authored a New York Times article called *How Companies Learn Your Secrets.* In it, he explains how Target data-mines

---

6   I am grossly oversimplifying the steps involved here

information about their customers' buying habits—all in order to make predictions about their future purchases. He relayed the story of a Target statistician named Andrew Pole and how he helped build Target's customer analysis engine:

As Pole's computers crawled through the data, he was able to identify about 25 products that, when analyzed together, allowed him to assign each shopper a "pregnancy prediction" score. More importantly, he could also estimate her due date to within a small window, so Target could send coupons timed to very specific stages of her pregnancy.

One Target employee I spoke to provided a hypothetical example. Take a fictional Target shopper named Jenny Ward, who is 23, lives in Atlanta and in March bought cocoa-butter lotion, a purse large enough to double as a diaper bag, zinc and magnesium supplements and a bright blue rug. There's, say, an 87 percent chance that she's pregnant and that her delivery date is sometime in late August.

This sounds crazy, but just wait. In one stunning real-life example of this very system at work a few years ago, Target assigned a high pregnancy score to a high-school student. The algorithm decided that, based on this high-schooler's shopping habits, there was a high likelihood that she was pregnant. So, their automated system started mailing her pregnancy-related promotions. Her father, understandably upset, walked into his local Minneapolis Target demanding answers. Duhigg writes:

"My daughter got this in the mail!" he said. "She's still in high school, and you're sending her coupons for baby clothes and cribs? Are you trying to encourage her to get pregnant?"

The manager didn't have any idea what the man was talking about. He looked at the mailer. Sure enough, it was addressed to the man's daughter and contained advertisements for maternity clothing, nursery furniture and pictures of smiling infants. The manager apologized and then called a few days later to apologize again.

On the phone, though, the father was somewhat abashed. "I had a talk with my daughter," he said. "It turns out there's been some activities in my house I haven't been completely aware of. She's due in August. I owe you an apology."

Like it or not, these analytics are happening everywhere, and not just on the internet. Your credit card number is its own real-world cookie, teaching your local Target or Walmart what you like and what you don't like every time you check out. In an extreme hypothetical example, once you check out, those stores can use video camera footage to reverse-engineer your path through the store, use eye-tracking equipment to measure what you looked at on the shelves, and use other cameras to measure your heart rate, breathing rate, and balance. All of it just from you walking through the store. Although this is a hypothetical example (after all, I don't work at Target or Walmart), this kind of technology is out there, and it *is* being used. Duhigg's article was written a decade ago—so there is ten years' worth of technological advancement that wasn't even in place when that high school student got pregnant.

Every time you walk through one of these stores, your shopping patterns are captured, fed into an artificial intelligence algorithm and repurposed to predict what you are going to do the next time you walk into the store.

Unlike Target or Walmart, however, sites like Amazon.com can use those predictions faster than just sending a piece of paper in the mail. Instead of inviting you to shop in a particular section of their store like Target does, Amazon *rearranges* the store as soon as you walk in. They place the things they think you want on the homepage or in the *Recommended Products* sections in the hopes that their computer was right and you add those items to your cart.

That's what a cookie helps with. And most of the time it is helpful—for example, I appreciate when Amazon recommends that I resupply some of my favorite snacks, or when there is a new book recommendation that I might like. But, as we've seen above, sometimes it can get a little creepy, so don't be surprised if you find a psychographic trait in this chapter that hits a bit too close to home. Despite the creepiness factor, it is critical for you to understand psychographics. They are not going to disappear any time soon and, even if you don't use them, your competitors will (and likely already are).

Behaviors

Behaviors are, as the title suggests, behavioral traits. They are based on cookie data that explains what any given person does on the internet (including where they go if they share GPS location on social media). Examples of behavioral traits are:

- People who prefer high-value goods
- Facebook payments users
- Facebook page admins
- Small business owners
- Anniversary coming up within 61-90 days
- Windows users

- Technology early adopters
- Expats
- Android users
- People with a 3G connection
- People with a 4G connection
- People who bought their first smartphone
- People who are interested in upcoming events
- Conservatives
- Liberals
- Moderates
- Engaged Shoppers
- Returned from travel 1 week ago
- Commuters
- Coffee shop regulars
- Fast food cravers
- Vegetarians & vegans
- Do-It-Yourselfers
- Fashionistas
- Pet lovers
- Thrill seekers
- Gamers
- TV Drama fans
- Avid news readers
- Bargain hunters
- Taxi service users

This is just the tip of the iceberg. There are thousands of behavioral segments that you can use to zone in on the exact group of people you want to reach. The Behavior psychographic trait alone can guide you to a very niche market very quickly. If you choose the right one, you'll have direct access to the people *most likely* to buy your product. When you combine Behaviors with the demographics that we've already reviewed, you can start to see how the two targeting methods (demographics and psychographics) work together to form uber-specific customer segments, such as *Single Gen X women with no kids who own a house, are in the top 25% of income earners, live in Chicago, speak English, use coffee shops frequently, and are likely to engage with Conservative political content.*

See how that gets incredibly specific?

Now, you sacrifice wider exposure as you start to add more and more targeting criteria. We will discuss finding the right level of specificity in the next chapter. For now, consider what Behavior attributes your audience has. You can use the list above, but that's a bit limited, and the available attributes are always changing based on new trends. I like to log into Google Ads and Facebook Ads to get inspiration around ways I can build my audience. Google will label Behaviors as *Affinity segments,* as shown in this screenshot of Google's ad manager:

SEARCH   BROWSE

←   What their interests and habits are

Affinity segments   ⌃

☐   Banking & Finance   ⌄

☐   Beauty & Wellness   ⌄

☐   Food & Dining   ⌄

☐   Home & Garden   ⌄

☐   Lifestyles & Hobbies   ⌄

☐   Media & Entertainment   ⌄

☐   News & Politics   ⌄

☐   Shoppers   ⌄

Facebook will label Behaviors in a similar way in their ads manager:

Q Add demographics, interests or behaviors	Suggestions **Browse**

▾ **Behaviors**   ❶

  ▹ Anniversary

  ▹ Consumer Classification

  ▹ Digital Activities

  ▹ Digital activities

  ▹ Expats

  ▹ Mobile Device User

  ▹ Mobile Device User/Device Use Time

  ▹ More Categories

Keep in mind that at this stage, I'm still *not* using these attributes for advertising purposes, but for audience planning purposes. Since the ad platforms have a vast array of Behaviors that you can browse, it is in your best interest to hop in there and have a look around.

Note: A common question at this point is "which platform should I look at—Google or Facebook?" Since we are **only** focusing on identifying your audience(s)—and not for advertising—you can look at both Facebook and Google for inspiration. We will go over how to use these Behavior attributes for advertising purposes later on.

Interests

Interests are different from Behaviors in that a person can self-label interests, whereas they cannot self-label Behaviors. This is almost the exclusive territory of Facebook, since Google doesn't have the kind of "like" button business model that Facebook does.

The "like" button drives most of the interest targeting on Facebook. Basically, if you "like" or "follow" a page on Facebook or a profile on Instagram, Facebook will take note and include you in the targeting for that particular interest. For example, if you decide to follow Tony Robbins on Facebook, you will start to see his posts, for sure, but you will also be targeted for ads being paid for by companies that want to get in front of people who like Tony Robbins. There are over 60 million Facebook pages in existence, so the choices are far and wide.

It is usually easy to come up with audience interests off the top of your head, but that is also an incomplete (and pretty random) process to follow. To help find your audience's interests, Facebook has created a tool called *Audience Insights.* Inside the Audience Insights panel, you can tell Facebook what you already know about your audience—your demographics and maybe a few interests or behaviors—and the tool will tell you more about that audience based on Facebook's data. I encourage you to explore the tool on your own—you're bound to learn a thing or two, even if you feel like you've got your head wrapped around your audience.

I'll show you how it works. First, we enter some basic audience information into the Audience Insights panel. For this demonstration, I will start with English speakers in the United States between 25 and 57 years old who HomeGoods and Whole Foods Market.

As I add these criteria to the search, the Audience Insights dashboard updates to tell me more about my audience:

Filter ×

Location

🔍 United States ×

Age

25 ▾ — 57 ▾

Gender

All ▾

Interests

🔍 Whole Foods Market ×

HomeGoods ×

Language

🔍 English (All) ×

See your audiences in Ads Manager

Create audience

Clear filters

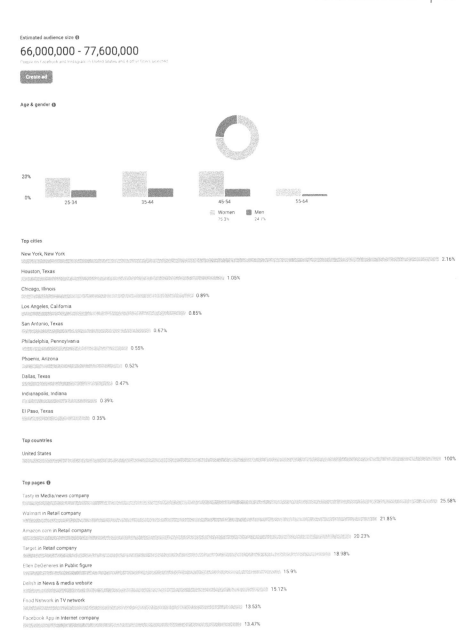

Estimated audience size

66,000,000 - 77,600,000

People on Facebook and Instagram in United States and 4 other filters selected

Create ad

Age & gender

Women 75.3%   Men 24.7%

Top cities

New York, New York — 2.16%
Houston, Texas — 1.05%
Chicago, Illinois — 0.89%
Los Angeles, California — 0.85%
San Antonio, Texas — 0.67%
Philadelphia, Pennsylvania — 0.55%
Phoenix, Arizona — 0.52%
Dallas, Texas — 0.47%
Indianapolis, Indiana — 0.39%
El Paso, Texas — 0.35%

Top countries

United States — 100%

Top pages

Tasty in Media/news company — 25.58%
Walmart in Retail company — 21.85%
Amazon.com in Retail company — 20.23%
Target in Retail company — 18.98%
Ellen DeGeneres in Public figure — 15.9%
Delish in News & media website — 15.12%
Food Network in TV network — 13.53%
Facebook App in Internet company — 13.47%

Do you see all that data? I can clearly see that, based on the little I know about my audience, they're concentrated most highly in New York City and most of them are between the ages of 35-54. But the most interesting data is at the bottom: the Facebook Pages section. This is a graph that shows the Facebook pages that your audience has a high likelihood of following. In this case, *Tasty,* *Walmart, Amazon.com, Target,* and *Ellen DeGeneres* are the top five.

Now you can cherry-pick which pages you feel best match your audience, feeding them right back into your original search, like this:

As you do that, the tool will update and give you even more specific data with new age distributions, locations, and page likes. You can do this until you've found a few interests that you normally wouldn't have thought of.

Combining Interests & Behaviors

It can get a little confusing to decide when to use Interests and when to use Behaviors. A good rule of thumb is to start with Behaviors first and then use Interests to add small tweaks to your audience.

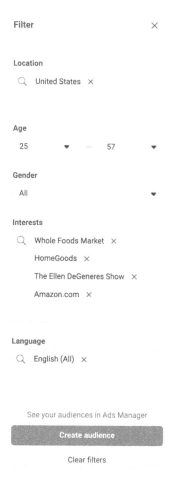

One example of this is an audience combination I've used many times for B2B audiences. I would start with the *small business owner* (all lowercase—capitalization is important in targeting land) Behavior and then add in specific interests that I expect the audience to have, such as popular influencers or software platforms. For example, an audience of small business owners who like Russell Brunson (an influencer in the marketing world and co-founder of ClickFunnels) will give me people who run their own business and have a high likelihood of using (or at least having an interest in) marketing funnels. Layering other interests on top of this audience, like HubSpot and Keap, would further narrow my audience to members of that audience who are highly familiar with (or use) specific software platforms.

Something to keep in mind…

At this point, it may feel like we're talking about how to create an ad campaign—but we're not. Remember, we are just trying to get clear on your audience. The tools we have at our disposal are mostly provided by ad platforms because they're the ones with the data. Years ago, it would have costed thousands of dollars to access the kind of data that Facebook and Google now make available for free. Why do they do it? Because they hope you'll think their data is better than everyone else's and you'll pay them to run ads. But that's not the stage we're at. Right now, were interested in defining your audience (also known as *market research)* and we're using every tool we have at our disposal.

Connections

Connections are another psychographic category led by Facebook. However, LinkedIn has developed robust capabilities around this as well. The Connections trait can be broken down into two main categories: Pages, Apps, Events, and Groups.

Pages

If I'm the administrator or owner of a Facebook Page or Instagram profile, I can reach people who have liked my page:

Audience
Define who you want to see your ads. Learn more

Create New Audience   Use Saved Audience ▾

Custom Audiences   Create new ▾

Engagement - Page

People who currently like or follow your Page: Vivid Labs

Q   Search existing audiences

Exclude

...*as well as* people who are likely to like my page:

Audience
Define who you want to see your ads. Learn more

Create New Audience   Use Saved Audience ▾

Custom Audiences   Create new ▾

Lookalike

Lookalike (AU, CA and 3 others, 1%) - People who currently like or follow you
r Page: Vivid Labs

Q Search existing audiences

Exclude

This is useful to know at this stage because if you know you can deliver an ad to someone who already knows who you are *and* likes the content you create, you will be able to craft messaging that takes that familiarity into consideration. You can use brand language, product names and other references that require a familiarity with your brand, such as a product update or launch announcement. These types of audiences are unique in that they are all *warmed up*—that is to say, they have had some level of experience with you in the past.

Apps & Events

The same thing is possible with people who have engaged with your app or a past event that you've hosted. For example, if you want to speak to a group of people who told Facebook they attended a conference you hosted (through a Facebook event) last year, you can write content directly for that audience—say, for a discounted early-bird ticket for past attendees or alumni.

Here's what that looks like in Facebook's ad targeting:

Connections

Add a connection type ▾

    Apps

        People who used your app

        People similar to those who used your app

        Exclude people who used your app

    Events

        People who responded to your event

        Exclude people who already responded to your event

        Advanced Combinations

You can also make advanced combinations of these audience attributes:

Advanced Combinations ▾

People who are connected to ⓘ

    🔍 Add a Page, app, or event

People similar to those who are connected to ⓘ

    🔍 Add a Page, or app

Exclude people who are connected to ⓘ

    🔍 Add a Page, app, or event

At the risk of beating a dead horse, I will repeat our purpose for this exercise: **right now, we are ONLY using these tools to get familiar with how specific your audience can be.** Once you complete the exercises in this chapter, we are going to exit the ads manager and other ad-related tools in order to assemble your campaign. Do NOT continue in the ad creation process at this point—despite the temptation.

Groups

Social media groups are an essential part of the social networking experience. They're also places that you can find and connect with members of your audience. In some cases, like Facebook, you can't serve advertisements to people based on the groups they are in. LinkedIn does allow you to do this. In either case, it's important to know what online forums your audience is spending time in. This gives you the ability to craft your marketing around people who are actively engaged in community discussions.

When someone is in a group, they have a higher likelihood of engaging with your content and have demonstrated a higher-than-average commitment to staying up to date with industry trends. A quick search of the job title "CTO" shows several LinkedIn groups with that term in the group name:

Who is your target audience?

Start building your audience by searching for attributes of professionals you want to reach   Close

⌂   Interests and Traits   Member Groups   Q CTO   ✕

☐ CTO Network

☐ CDO/CIO/CTO Leadership Council

☐ Chief Executives | CEO, COO, CFO, CTO & CXO's (Startups, Investors, Blockchain & Dealflow)

☐ Linkin CTOs and VPs Engineering

☐ CIO Exchange - CIO, CTO, CISO, CDO, CAO

☐ The Linked CXO / President, CEO, COO, CIO, CTO, MD, VP, Director 's

Now I can craft messaging around CTOs with a willingness to (1) keep up with their industry, (2) build their reputation through community engagement, and (3) learn from others in their profession.

If I was planning a marketing campaign around an upcoming IT conference, I would form my audience around those CTO groups. Doing so would guarantee that my audience is made up of CTOs who are highly engaged and open to discussions around their industry. Knowing this, I would have more confidence in focusing my campaign messaging on terms and topics that CTOs would resonate with. Group targeting, in this case, is incredibly valuable.

MINIMUM VIABLE AUDIENCE

Now that we've reviewed demographics and psychographics, you have a better idea of how specific you can get when creating your audience. But now comes the murky part—figuring out exactly how specific you *should* be.

Generally speaking, the more specific your audience targeting is, the fewer people your audience will contain. If you are too specific, your campaign won't reach enough people, and if you are too wide in your targeting, your campaign won't convert your audience. So, the question becomes—*how specific should you be when identifying your audience?*

There are actually two sides to this question. The first side has to do with your *planning audience* and the second side has to do with your *advertising audience*. Your planning audience informs your campaign messaging, from your headlines to your video scripts. Your advertising audience has to do with the targeting criteria you load into ad platforms when you are buying media[7], from social media ads to billboards. That particular audience changes more frequently and responds to changing seasons and trends, while your planning audience is more stable.

In this section of the book, we are dealing with your planning audience **only.** We are concerned with understanding who your customers are—not how to reach them on any given ad platform. When it comes to deciding on the level of specificity for your first planning audience, I like to stick with what I call the *minimum viable level of specificity.*

What does that mean?

It means that when you are going through this exercise, especially for the first time, you should focus on the largest audience possible while also maintaining a high-enough level of specificity (between your demographics and psychographics)

---

7   *Media buying* is a marketing term that just means paying for advertising.

to guarantee that your audience contains people that have a higher-than-average likelihood of buying your product. I call this the *minimum viable audience (MVA)*. For example, the MVA for a Ford dealership could be Millennials who (1) are in the top 50% of income earners nationwide, (2) graduated from college, (3) live within a 30-mile radius of the dealership location, (4) recently got a new job, and (5) have an interest in cars.

After you go through this exercise for the first time, you can add more attributes to your MVA to create a *secondary audience (SA)*, such as being a new parent. So, whereas the MVA would include the five characteristics outlined above, the SA would include six characteristics—the same five from the MVA plus the characteristic of being a new parent. The addition of that sixth characteristic further refines your audience, thus making it smaller, but more reactive to certain language around parenting. For example, that SA would allow you to craft content focused on having a newborn being carried around in a minivan or SUV.

Exercise: The Audience Assembly (Creating Your MVA)

It's time to create your first MVA. The worksheet provided at the link below will guide you through the creation of a Customer Briefing. This is a simple exercise that allows you to document your MVA's characteristics, including their demographics and psychographics. From there, you can add more secondary characteristics to create your secondary audiences. The process of creating your Customer Briefing is called an *Audience Assembly*.

To get the free Customer Briefing worksheet, go to **heydanrussell.com/snakeoil**

Assignment: Schedule Your Audience Assemblies

It's now time to make space in your calendar to host bi-annual Audience Assemblies to continually revisit your audience characteristics. These are 60-minute meetings with your team (or, if you are a solo founder, a spot on your calendar) to build a new Customer Briefing. It's important that you hold these twice a year. Holding it more often would mess with your ongoing marketing campaign efforts (which we'll be installing into your marketing operating system soon) and holding it less often would lead to you missing important evolutions in your audience. These bi-annual meetings also provide a forum for creating your secondary audiences, which will become the focus of marketing campaigns to come.

To get a downloadable agenda for your Audience Assembly, head to **heydan-russell.com/snakeoil**

After you've completed your first Audience Assembly, schedule another one for six months from now and set your calendar to repeat that event every six months. Once you've done that, you'll be ready to move on to the next stage of building your marketing operating system: your Campaigns.

8   WHAT'S A MARKETING CAMPAIGN (REALLY?)

W e've now moved into the second stage of your marketing operating system. Now that you have completed your first Audience Assembly, you have a clear idea of who you will be marketing to. You are now ready to plan your first campaign.

Consider how a marketing campaign was described 30 years ago. A "campaign" was a collection of direct mailers, print ads, radio spots, and TV commercials all revolving around the nucleus of a core message. The campaign was designed to reach a company's minimum viable audience or secondary audience across multiple channels. With enough time and exposure, those mailers, ads, radio spots, and commercials would lead to a higher level of sales.

That was fifty years ago.

Today, our definition of "marketing campaign" has changed. Unless you're paying a huge agency, a *marketing campaign* these days is much narrower in scope than it was a few years ago. Campaigns these days are usually limited to a single ad platform and a few email broadcasts. Hardly a large, coordinated effort.

There is a good reason for this. Marketing has become so complicated in recent years that businesses have been forced to make sacrifices for the sake of budget and time. Small businesses, in particular, don't have the resources or the expertise to launch a full-fledged campaign, so they eliminate the complicated options and end up jumping on the most popular bandwagons—like Facebook and Google.

According to eMarketer, those two platforms alone account for over 56.8% of total money spent on pay-per-click advertising. They are big businesses, and they are both built on getting other businesses to pay them money to run ads. So, it is not surprising that they have spent a lot of time and money convincing other businesses that the whole marketing process can live inside their ecosystem. Essentially, they have slowly indoctrinated people (especially entrepreneurs) to skip the whole "strategy" process and dive right into hitting that *Boost* button on their posts. Five bucks here, ten bucks there, a nice bump in engagement, and before long, you're sitting in front of a slot machine wondering why one thing works and the next thing doesn't.

A marketing campaign doesn't begin with the *Create Campaign* button in your ads manager.

It begins with the process we just completed over the last few chapters—finding your customers—and continues with the creation of a well-planned marketing campaign. That campaign (and not the platforms) will dictate where and when your content will appear, as well as whether it will appear in a paid advertisement at all.

So *back off*, big tech. We've got work to do before you're invited to the table.

The Purpose of a Marketing Campaign

A campaign is designed to do… what, exactly?

If you answered, *"Make sales, duh!"* then I'm sorry—you are dead wrong. The next few paragraphs will change your mind.

The purpose of a marketing campaign is to generate *attention*. It is the job of the Conversions side of the marketing operating system to turn that attention into sales. We haven't gotten there yet—but we're getting closer.

See, most people, when building a marketing campaign, tend to blur the lines between *attention* and *conversion*. They have dollar signs in their eyes and try to pack all kinds of copywriting best-practices into just one ad, leading to a jumbled frenzy of mixed messages. Unless you are a highly experienced copywriter or video marketer, if you are trying to sell someone directly from an ad, that means you aren't trying to capture the person's attention. So, all of your hard selling work is for nothing. You spent your whole 0.18 seconds in their news feed trying to stuff something down their throat rather than actually speaking to them. This is one of the reasons why most people see 5,000 ads in a single day[8] and, at the end of the day, can't tell you what even *one* of them said.

AIDA is an age-old marketing acronym that stands for *Attention, Interest, Desire, Action*. It describes the basic mental steps that someone must complete before buying something. It's basic, but useful.

---

8   Story, Louise. "Anywhere the Eye Can See, It's Likely to See an Ad." The New York Times, The New York Times, 15 Jan. 2007, www.nytimes.com/2007/01/15/business/media/15everywhere.html.

Do you notice anything interesting about the order of the steps?

Ah, yes—Attention comes first!

Not Interest. Not Desire. Not Action.

Attention.

These days, attention is hard to come by. With all those ads appearing in front of our faces every day, we've learned to tune out everything but the most urgent or relevant of messages. If that message happens to be an ad, we put it through another rigorous split-second process where our lizard brains decide whether it is exciting enough to stick around for. This is why attention now comes at a premium.

Celebrity marketer (yes, I just said that) Gary "Vee" Vaynerchuk is known for his colorful tirades about hustle, marketing, and dedication to the #entrepreneurlife movement, often saying that he's good at what he does because the #1 thing he focuses on is "day-trading attention."

He's not wrong.

His agency, VaynerMedia, produces marketing for the likes of Mint Mobile, Shell, Subway, PepsiCo, Johnson & Johnson, Unilever, and TikTok. One thing they do better than a lot of agencies is predict where attention is going. This is what Gary means by *day-trading attention.* He and his agency know, better than most, how much attention is worth in different places for different people.

One of the reasons that sales funnels and split testing and all kinds of nifty, shiny marketing training programs have become so popular over the last few years is because most of us have stopped capturing our own customers' attention in favor of easier marketing projects. While solopreneurs get distracted by working on the other three steps of AIDA, guys like Gary are swooping in with marketing that captures attention in a noisy, noisy world. The secret is that once you've captured attention, you can easily beat your competitors on the *Interest, Desire,* and *Action* steps. Because once you have Attention, you have trust.

So why do businesses end up skipping the *Attention* step?

Because the other three are safer. They're more measured. There are more trainings to help us get *better* at everything *but* capturing attention—because attention has become really difficult to come by. In a nutshell, most businesses skip the attention step because it's too *hard* and *confusing.*

Why is it hard and confusing? Because attention is the only step of the marketing process that demands something that most businesses haven't quite figured out:

Telling.
Great.
Stories.
And this, my friend, is the single reason why marketing campaigns exist.
To tell great stories.

WHAT'S THE BIG IDEA?

We've already visited the concept of a Big Idea earlier in this book. The Big Idea is the driving force of your marketing campaign and the story (or stories) it's telling. It's also the most abstract part of the marketing operating system. It requires the most creativity. So, we're going to take it step by step in order to help you come up with your own Big Idea.

The first thing we need to do is ask the question: *What IS a Big Idea?*

Think back to Don Draper and the marketing pitch for Kodak's Carousel machine. Remember how smoothly the concept landed? When Don finished his monologue and the lights turned back on, the Kodak executives were sitting dumbfounded in their chairs. Remember the feeling? The feeling of *"I didn't expect THAT…"*

The idea that the Carousel was more than just a slide projector *blew their minds.* They felt something. Don's pitch stirred something deep inside them. It was like watching a commercial and getting the feeling that it had a *soul.* Like the Carousel was reaching out and saying to them: *you can have nostalgia on-demand.*

That's a Big Idea.

For the Carousel, it's *nostalgia on demand.*

For Procter & Gamble's Mother's Day ad, it was *"mom is a hero.'*

For Dove's Campaign for Real Beauty, it's *"we're all beautiful."*

For Nike's Colin Kaepernick campaign, it's *"believe in something, no matter the cost."*

It seems simple, doesn't it? To boil such an emotional journey into just a few words? Yet, it's not simple. It's exceptionally complex. As the French philosopher Blaise Pascal once said, "I would have written a shorter letter, but I did not have the time," brevity and simplicity come at a high cost. A simple Big Idea from any company carried a heavy price tag.

But it's not a price tag that can be measured in dollars; this is what makes the Big Idea so powerful. It can be leveraged just as easily by a broke twenty-year-old as it can by a multinational corporation. It's pure creativity—but pure creativity is hard to come by. You need to know how to harness it. It requires you to take a risk. To do something you might not be comfortable with. This is what separates successful and unsuccessful marketers. The power of the Big Idea can be harnessed by anybody, and just one Big Idea can lead to fortunes.

And yet, the Big Idea is fragile.

It is the easiest part of the marketing process to ignore. It won't come looking for you. It won't tell you, *"hey, you forgot about me…"* It will just silently float by along with the promise of a killer marketing campaign. So you need to know how to harness it—you need a tool to come up with a Big Idea of your own.

The Big Idea Brainstorm

I've tried all kinds of different ways to come up with Big Ideas for my clients over the years, from copywriting templates to drinking copious amounts of whiskey. None of it works as well as the *Big Idea Brainstorm.*

In a Big Idea Brainstorm, you sit down with a pad of paper and go through question prompts that will force you to look at your business and your product in different ways—from the perspective of your customers, their customers, their friends, and so on.

There are several prompts that I use to spur new ideas in a Big Idea Brainstorm—we'll go over a few of them soon—but one of my favorites is this:

If your product had a voice, and it could talk, what would it say to your prospective customers?

Just thinking in a quiet space about this question will lead you to places you've never been before. It will get you *thinking differently* about your product. About your customers.

(Also, are you starting to see why having your MVA ready from the beginning is so important?)

The Big Idea Brainstorm (BIB for short) is a simple, delicate, and potent exercise that focuses your mind on accomplishing one task: coming up with an original marketing concept that can form the nucleus of your marketing campaign.

Fortunately, instead of sitting in front of a blank piece of paper, you have this book. And in a little bit, I am going to give you the prompts that will help guide you through the BIB. Pay close attention to how the questions and prompts are phrased. Think about them before writing. Make copies if you need to. Grab a pen and write in your own notebook.

This is your creative space. Your mind's art studio. Your mental workshop. Do what you need to in order to get into the right frame of mind—I personally prefer to do my creative work in the morning, but I also use meditation to get into a creative mood. If magic mushrooms or a glass of wine in the evening get your creative juices flowing, go for it. Whatever you need to do.

The one thing I will alert you to—before you dive in—is that this process may seem uncomfortable. Even painful.

It's not often that we sit down and examine our product from the perspectives offered by this exercise. You may find yourself questioning the value of your product. You may find that you can't come up with any good ideas. You might even feel that nobody in your audience wants to hear from you.

When you encounter these moments, it's critically important to **push through it.** Those moments of stress and pain and uncertainty are moments that scare most other people away from looking into the soul of their marketing. That is what separates you, who are sitting and reading this book, from everyone else. Always keep in mind that *you* are the best person to come up with your own company's Big Idea.

So who better *than you* to go through this exercise?

Who better *than you* to have a creative streak that inspires a new way of thinking about your product?

Who better *than you* to form a more intimate connection with your customers? To create a mental melting pot of words and ideas that add up to a feeling that no other brand can create?

Big Ideas don't come easy. No pressure, no diamonds. But the rewards are well worth it.

Ready to go?

Let's get at it.

Exercise: The Big Idea Brainstorm (BIB)

It's important to keep in mind that, for every business, there can be many, many, many Big Ideas. In most cases, there are as many Big Ideas as there are secondary audiences. Basically, if there is a more specific group of people you can speak to, there is a more specific message you can send to them.

The trick is sitting down to come up with that message. That is exactly what we are going to do in the BIB. If this is your first time, you will be crafting a Big Idea around your MVA (Minimum Viable Audience). Big Ideas built around an MVA are more generally accepted, which usually means they align closely with the mission or slogan of the company itself. For example, the MVA Big Idea for the North Face is *Never Stop Exploring*. This is the same as the company's actual slogan; you'll find that same pattern with companies that have well-established brands. They can use their MVA Big Idea as the driving force for all their brand-building efforts.

Unless you have an extremely well-established brand, odds are you haven't yet figured out your MVA Big Idea. If you *do* have an extremely well-established brand, and you *do* know your MVA Big Idea, then continue with this exercise by pursuing a Secondary Audience Big Idea (*SA Big Idea*). This is a Big Idea that would be used for a campaign targeted at one of your secondary audiences (in the case of a flower shop, a secondary audience would be newly engaged couples).

Whichever audience you are pursuing a Big Idea for (MVA or SA), the process is the same:

Step One: Find a quiet spot to sit down

Step Two: Get your head right. Do what you need to do to eliminate distractions and get focused.

Step Three: Pull out a journal, stack of blank pages, sketch pad, or some other physical (non-digital) writing mechanism.

Step Four: Begin to write the answers to the prompts below on the pages now in front of you.

Big Idea Brainstorm Prompts

Note: In order to avoid redundancy, I'm using the term "product" below as an umbrella term that includes both products and services. Whatever it is that your company sells, that is what I refer to as your "product."

- If your product had a voice, and it could talk, what would it say to your prospective customers?
- What is one thing you know AND your customers know about your product or industry—but neither of you talk about it openly?
- If your product was a cartoon character, which character would it be and what would its catchphrase be?

- What is one thing about your industry that really annoys your customers?
- Why do your customers buy from you instead of your competitors?
- In one word, what is a specific and positive emotion your customers experience when using your product? (Try to avoid terms that are too general—be specific and creative)
- What phrase might go through your customers' minds when they use your product for the first time?
- What do your customers desire above all else, even beyond your product's immediate and obvious benefits?
- What do your customers fear? What are they concerned about? What insecurities do they have?
- If your best friend was a customer and you were sitting at a campfire, what would they admit to you is the real reason they need your product?

You can get a printable copy of these prompts at **heydanrussell.com/snake-oil**

Reading this list of prompts for the first time may seem like another pie-in-the-sky exercise. But like I said before—**stick with it.** Each of these prompts is designed to get you thinking about your product and your customer from a specific perspective. These perspectives are what allow you to navigate around your own biases—allow you to "see the forest for the trees," as they say—and potentially discover new ways to describe your product and talk about your customers' challenges and desires.

The BIB inside your Marketing Operating System

I've included the Big Idea Brainstorm exercise above to help get your creative juices flowing before we move into the campaign creation process in the next chapter. But in the future, the BIB exercise will be incorporated into your overall campaign planning process during your Campaign Creation Meeting. So right now, there's no need to schedule your BIBs. We'll take care of that later.

THE CAMPAIGN CAR WASH
PART 1: STYLE

Let's take a second to recap—and celebrate.

So far in this book, you've built your Minimum Viable Audience (MVA) and spent the time and effort to come up with your first Big Idea. Nice work! Seriously.

This is not an easy process. Some people, by this point, have said "screw this, I thought this was going to be a motivational marketing book!"

Sorry. Wrong guy.

Right now, you are going way deeper than just deciding what social media platform to use. You are answering the deeper questions and getting answers that will guide you for years to come.

Allllright. Let's keep moving.

Now that you have your MVA and your Big Idea, you can start moving to the next step of building your Campaign—the content!

What do I mean by "content?"

The content of your campaign is the meat of your marketing. It is your Big Idea manifested in a tangible form, like written content and video content. Most times, businesses create content for the sake of creating content (i.e., busywork). This is not what I'm talking about. Having a content *strategy* means that every word you write and every video you create has a purpose. It means that, when you publish your content, it combines to form a **campaign** that serves a specific purpose beyond just filling up your audience's news feeds or email inboxes.

The campaign creation process is like going through a car wash—you have to go through a few steps, like moving from the soap to the wax to the rinse to the dryers. I call it the Campaign Car Wash. Each step is focused on building the right content that will drive your campaign—each step is critical and cannot be skipped. The steps to the Campaign Car Wash are:

1. Content Style
2. Content Medium

3. Content Exposure

By the time you've finished the process, you'll have turned an abstract Big Idea into a squeaky-clean, hyper-specific content strategy that feeds your overall business goals.

So let's get to it.

The first stop in the Campaign Car Wash is figuring out your content's style. The style of your campaign's content dictates the type of energy that your campaign exhibits. This is related to your brand—if you have a very technical or "nerdy" brand, an educational style might be most appropriate for you. There are three main style categories that content fits into:

1. Educational
2. Inspirational
3. Entertaining

As you read through the next three chapters, you'll begin to visualize the style, or the energy, that your content can exhibit. Try not to get stuck in exactly what the content will look like. We will review that in a few chapters during Part 2 of the Campaign Car Wash. For now, focus only on the style of your content—its energy, its vibe, its tone, however you prefer to think of it. We'll translate that into real-world formats soon enough.

EDUCATIONAL CONTENT

Educational content is built to share information that your audience would not otherwise think of or be able to access themselves. In 1951, David Ogilvy published his first-ever ad. It was called the *Guinness Guide to Oysters*. In it, he showed nine illustrations of different types of oysters, explaining how each of them paired well with a glass of Guinness beer.

This was the first ad of its kind. It immediately catapulted Ogilvy into the heavy-hitter marketing club. The reason it performed so well is that, unlike other beer ads, the *Guinness Guide to Oysters* educated beer fans by sharing a fact that they probably weren't aware of—that Guinness, although it is a beer, compliments the taste of oysters in a unique way. This was useful and actionable information that had a direct tie-in to the decision of whether to drink Guinness, and it expanded the universe of possible situations in which someone *could* order a Guinness. It also had the added effect of creating curiosity around what an oyster paired with a Guinness would taste like.

Educational content is not about just blasting your audience with random information. It is not about creating how-to videos or instructional whitepapers on how great your product is. Instead, high-quality Educational content presents an idea that your audience has never thought about before. It illustrates possibilities that they would not have considered on their own. As a result, it has the potential to communicate your Big Idea in a creative and out-of-the-box way.

If you feel this is the right style of content for you, start thinking about ways that your audience can incorporate your product into their lives, specifically in ways they haven't thought of before. Going back to my trusty flower shop example, if I were to create a high-quality piece of Educational content, I would share the story of a husband giving his wife flowers "just because." That phrase—*just because*—could be the Big Idea that powers an entire campaign. You can probably imagine that phrase on a billboard or at the end of a TV commercial, right? Remember—Big Ideas are simple but *powerful*.

Your Educational content can be just as emotionally engaging and deeply felt as the other two types of content style. It is up to you to leverage your Big Idea in a creative way that causes people to think, *"hmm... I've never thought of that."*

INSPIRATIONAL CONTENT

Inspirational content is designed to lead your audience to change their beliefs around a given topic. You see a lot of Inspirational content from companies that are trying to get you out of your comfort zone or routine. Theme restaurants, amusement parks, and vacation destinations all fall into this category. Their content is designed to push you to believe you can do something you've never done, go somewhere you've never visited, or feel something you've never experienced before (or thought was out of reach at this point in your life). Out of the three styles, Inspirational content is by far the most emotionally impactful.

AncestryDNA has some of the most effective Inspirational content I've ever found. In one ad campaign named *The DNA Journey*, members of the AncestryDNA team gathered a group of people together for a DNA heritage study. Most of the members of this group ardently believed they were direct descendants of their home country (such as 100% English or 100% Icelandic). During a few short interviews, they shared that they were either better than, or more favorable than, some other ethnicities. One man from Bangladesh suggested that he had a negative view of people from India and Pakistan due to cultural clashes.

When asked by the AncestryDNA team if they would be open to a DNA study, a few participants showed signs of insecurity—as if they felt like their reality was about to change. If you watch the ad on YouTube, you can see it in their faces. The uncertainty—the fear. Then the video fast-forwards two weeks, and we see the entire group gathered in the same room. Each participant is called up, one at a time, to read their AncestryDNA results. And each person, one by one, stares in shock at their results. They each discover that, not only is their heritage traced back to all kinds of countries outside their home country, but in many cases, they share a common ancestry with the same countries for which they expressed their disdain, or even hatred.

AncestryDNA created this Inspirational content from one Big Idea that could be summarized as *"we're all connected."* They broke down political and emotional walls that had been built up for decades in these peoples' lives. And they did it in a manner of seconds by using science and objectivity. To see this unfold in a video is an incredibly inspiring experience, and AncestryDNA knew that. That's the business they're in. They wanted to get their audience to believe they are more connected with the world than they thought, and their content accomplished that goal.

Inspirational content is not easy to create, and it can come in many different forms. But there is one common thread that you can find in all types of Inspirational content—demonstration. By demonstrating the Big Idea at the core of your message, regardless of the format, you can show your audience what is possible. This, slowly but surely, causes them to consider a belief they had never considered before. They can do this because the content itself provides proof that the belief is **valid** and **attainable**. Without this proof, your content won't hold your audience's attention. They will dismiss the belief as either unattainable or invalid.

For your content to inspire, it must prove that the belief is within reach of your audience. AncestryDNA did this by showing customers' experiences with their product. The TOMS apparel company, widely known for its Buy One Give One business model, did this through their *For One, Another* campaign (TOMS gives out a free pair of shoes with every pair that is purchased). This campaign was built on the Big Idea that *buying shoes is not just about you,* and the belief they inspired in their audience was that *buying a piece of clothing can improve humanity.* Through their TV ads, they *showed* their customers the kind of impact that occurs when they buy a pair of TOMS shoes. In short, they provided proof that the belief was valid and attainable. Just buy a pair of TOMS shoes and you can have an impact.

There are a few helpful forms of demonstration that you can use in your Inspirational content. The first is a story. AncestryDNA shared stories of customer experiences with their product. It was straightforward, yet intense.

Another form of demonstration is simply *showing* people the evidence. TOMS demonstrated their Buy One Give One business model through simple video clips. They showed people buying a new pair of TOMS shoes, and then they showed a new pair of shoes being given to a child in a third-world country. It was simple, yet effective. By showing the video clips of children in need receiving new shoes, TOMS proved the belief that *buying a piece of clothing can improve humanity* was valid. And by demonstrating that buying a pair of shoes can make it all happen, the audience could easily conclude that the belief was attainable.

A third form of proof is an authority figure. The AFL (Australian Football League) released a campaign called *I'd Like To See That* in which they advocated for more women playing in pro sports. The Big Idea of the campaign was *"There should be more female athletes competing in sports."* In order to get their audience to really commit to this Big Idea, the AFL brought in celebrity athletes to share their own eagerness for more women to go pro. The effect of hearing this message repeated in different ways by all these highly authoritative figures in sports was that the audience began to take the Big Idea seriously, which accomplishes the goal of proving it's valid. Then, by playing clips of real female athletes competing and winning in soccer (football, if you're outside the US) matches, the audience saw that it was already happening—proving the Big Idea is *attainable*.

There are all kinds of ways you can provide proof that your belief is valid and attainable. Telling stories, showing the proof, and using authority figures are just three out of many methods of proof you can provide. Regardless of which form of proof you use, it is critical to ensure that your proof shows the audience that the belief you want them to hold is both valid and attainable.

Hashtag Activism

At any given moment, there are trending topics in the world. You can see them on any social media platform, and they almost always have a hashtag. Popular trends in recent years have led to the term "hashtag activism" being used to describe the most powerful and popular trends. Such trends have been shared widely across social media, including #MeToo, #BlackLivesMatter, #BringBack-OurGirls, #IceBucketChallenge, #TakeAKnee, and #NeverAgain.

When you can align your brand with a movement that is taking the world by storm, you can not only tie your brand into a message that has a higher chance of being shared, but you also contribute to a movement that has the potential to change the world. This is the best of both worlds—a chance for your marketing to be successful *and* support an important cultural movement that needs as much exposure as it can get.

An important note to make here is that Hashtag Activism content should not be used as a carrier for direct product promotion. If you were to make a social media post in support of #MeToo, for example, the last thing you want to do is run a sale alongside it. It is in poor taste, and it is obvious that you are just trying to make money from a movement that is tied to women's rights. What you can do, though, is position your brand as taking a stand *with* those who are fighting the good fight. This is an excellent way to reinforce your campaign's Big Idea while contributing to a worthy movement.

While it's in poor taste to directly promote your products while engaging in hashtag activism, there *is* a way to boost your company's reach. One way to authentically integrate your product into a movement like this is to host a charity event or fundraiser. I've done this myself. We recently had the misfortune, as a global community, of seeing the complete collapse of the Afghanistan government. The Taliban took control of the country over the span of a single week, throwing the country into complete disarray. Alongside the political crisis rose another crisis of a humanitarian nature. Now that the Taliban were in control of the country, women were at particularly high risk of being persecuted.

In an effort to do our part, I had my company launch a charity workshop. I told my audience that 100% of proceeds would be donated to the Women for Afghan Women charity. I had to be very careful and upfront that Vivid Labs was *not* interested in making any money from this event—that every penny would be donated to charity. But, importantly, it was a way that we as a company could drive awareness and desire for people to donate to a worthy cause. I knew that posting about this charity workshop would help drive awareness of the issue, and the fact that we could provide something of value to encourage people to donate helped to align the whole initiative to our brand and core value of *Go Beyond*. We made no money, but we did help make money for a worthy cause, and my audience was reminded of what my company's brand stood for.

You will find that, depending on the movement you choose to support, you may invite criticism. This is a good thing. Nike caught a lot of flak for their Colin Kaepernick campaign supporting the #TakeAKnee movement. People posted videos of them burning their Nike shoes, boycotting Nike, and so on. Nike didn't care. They were in it for the long haul and knew that, according to their brand values, they needed to tell the world where they stood.

As movements like this arise, think carefully about how you can help spread the word. There are millions of people sharing, posting, and engaging with content around important cultural issues. Hashtag Activism gives you, as a company, an incredible opportunity to do your part in standing your ground on an important topic. The long-term result of this is that, as Nike experienced, your customers will feel that they know you better, and they will be more loyal as a result.

ENTERTAINING CONTENT

Entertaining content is the next style that can drive your content strategy. This style can be found on all kinds of sites like YouTube, TikTok, Instagram, Facebook, and Snapchat. The major differentiator of Entertaining content is that it is designed to keep your audience's attention using comedy or drama. Entertaining content incorporates, at its most basic level, a level of curiosity and storytelling that doesn't necessarily need to convince an audience to change their beliefs (as Inspirational content does) and doesn't need to share information (as Educational content does). Its sole purpose is to share a story or message that is, at its most basic level, entertaining.

A good example of Entertaining content is late night talk show clips on YouTube. If you search for Conan O'Brien or Jimmy Kimmel on YouTube, you'll find vast troves of clips from their shows. They will all be focused on a particular moment on the show, such as a clip from a celebrity interview or a "remote" segment in which they take the cameras to another location to film. Talk shows can draw from a 30-minute or 60-minute episode and create dozens of these clips at a time. The goal is to get people to *watch more,* which builds loyalty and trust.

Another example of Entertaining content is YouTube content creator MrBeast. He produces videos that are crazy and awe-inspiring. In one video that has amassed just short of 100 million views on YouTube, he buys $600,000 worth of fireworks and sets them all off at the same time, setting a new world record. He's not trying to inspire or educate his audience, but instead he's trying to entertain them and have fun. The fact that his video (and channel) has built such a large following is a testament to how successful this strategy can be—not to mention profitable, because MrBeast got paid by YouTube for every one of those 100 million video views.

But Entertaining content can go beyond just high-volume consumption. It can also be used to present a product in a favorable light, support important cultural movements, create viral content, and build highly immersive experiences for audiences looking for deeper methods of brand engagement. Whereas the other two styles of content (Educational and Inspirational) rely on a deeper connection between the brand and the audience, Entertaining content makes use of instinctual mental and behavioral patterns. When people encounter this type of content, the universal psychological response is to pay attention and engage. Let's look at four popular categories of Entertaining content that help brands achieve this goal.

Product Placements

In 2019, global product placement investment rose by 14.5% to an all-time high of $20.6 billion. The COVID pandemic put a temporary lull in this market in 2020—and I say *temporary* because estimates are, according to PQ Media, that investment is poised to rise 13.8% to $23.3 billion globally. This is fast growth for an industry segment that traditionally relied on movies and TV shows to do their work.

The reason for this rapid growth is something called *influencer* marketing. By teaming up with social media influencers (people with huge followings on platforms like Instagram and TikTok), companies can promote their products to their audiences in a new way. Influencer marketing has taken off in popularity as consumers have gotten more tech-savvy and have started filtering out traditional advertising. According to Deloitte's Ad Blocking Media Report, three-quarters of North Americans have some kind of ad blocker on their browser, which means that traditional paid media will not be displayed on their computers.

Influencers bypass this problem by talking about a product directly in their social media posts, none of which are paid. There are levels to this market—for example, you can use an influencer marketing platform like UpFluence to find a social media influencer with a following that matches your audience and pay them a couple hundred dollars to make a post about your product.

Alternatively, as an example, if you have the budget and your audience matches his, you can pay Dwayne Johnson $1 million to make a post about your product. If he is not quite your audience's style, maybe Kylie Jenner would be a better fit. Her posts run about the same price tag. But—and this is a big *but*—you must convince *them* that your product is amazing, is the right fit for your audience, and will help them build their following, not tarnish their reputation.

This is the big kicker of influencer marketing—finding the right person to do the promoting. If you follow Dwayne Johnson, you know that he talks a lot about exercise and his tequila company, and he has a funny-meets-tough kind of style. If your brand or product doesn't line up with his brand, don't even bother asking.

This is the big mistake that a lot of product placement campaigns make—not achieving alignment with the brand of the influencer or piece of content in which the product is placed.

Some of the best product placements in history are iconic because they are integrated seamlessly into the plot or brand of the content itself. James Bond's Aston Martin is a long-running example of a successful brand partnership. It's a win-win for Aston Martin as well as Metro-Goldwyn-Mayer—Aston gets brand exposure while MGM gets an iconic car that audiences love to see Bond return to.

Another classic example can be found in Steven Spielberg's movie *E.T.* Before filming the movie, Spielberg knew that he needed a way for Elliot to lure E.T. into his room. He had the idea of using a trail of candy for E.T. to follow, so he approached the Mars candy company with the opportunity to feature M&Ms in the movie. Mars famously turned Spielberg down, leading him to bring the same offer to Hershey, who owned Reese's Pieces. They accepted the offer and Spielberg wrote Reese's Pieces into the script, leading to one of the most classic scenes from the movie. After the release of E.T., sales of Reese's Pieces increased by about 300%.

The point here is that product placements typically don't work unless there's a *reason* for the product to be in the content in the first place. James Bond's Aston Martin and E.T.'s Reese's Pieces are both highly integrated products without which the movies' plots wouldn't have worked as well.

It is imperative that you take the same approach with your own influencer product placement. We reviewed above how product placement can be successful in traditional media like movies and TV shows. But in the world of influencer marketing, the question moves from *"how do we integrate the product into the content?"* to *"how do we integrate the product into the influencer's brand?"*. Answering this question first will save you time and money in your product placement content.

Viral Content

There was a massive power outage during the 2013 Super Bowl in New Orleans. For a full 30 minutes, the entire stadium went dark, and the game was paused. Massive uncertainty ensued. People wondered what was happening,

Everyone's imagination started painting pictures of the countless people on the engineering staff running around like crazy in the stadium's electrical room.

But there was another team running around during those 30 minutes. They were in the Oreo Cookie offices running marketing mission control for the game. As soon as the power outage occurred, their team was already in place to respond. They whipped together an image with an Oreo cookie surrounded by darkness. They wrote a caption that said, *"you can still dunk in the dark,"* and they posted it on Twitter.

Within seconds, the tweet began to get shared. By the time the lights came back on in the stadium, it had gone viral. People loved the tongue-in-cheek humor, the fast response time, and the on-brand messaging (everyone knows what "dunk" means in the context of an Oreo cookie). As a result, Oreo got over 13,000 retweets and massive brand exposure.

Producing viral content is not an easy feat and a lot of brands get caught in the trap of relying on rising trends to do the heavy lifting—as if any post with the trend's hashtag will get thousands of retweets within seconds. This just isn't true. There are 132,000,000 results on Google for the term *"how to write a viral post."* There are 207 books on Amazon for the term *"viral marketing."* I can't stress enough how much content is out there which tries to encapsulate the formula for viral content. The truth is that there is no formula worth pursuing. Your brand's style is always going to interact with different trends in different ways. There are patterns, however, that warrant investigation, and they all come down to how viral posts are measured—and that is the number of times a post has been shared.

One of the biggest levers to viral marketing is getting social media influencers to share your content. Although "social media influencer" doesn't have a specific definition, they all have loyal followings and high engagement. You don't need to have millions of followers to be an influencer in the same way that you don't need an audience of millions of people in order to make millions of dollars. If you can get an influencer with a loyal following to share your post, you will have taken the first step to going viral. According to AgencySparks, if a social media influencer shares your post, it will receive 32% more shares. If three influencers share your post, it will receive 200% more shares. And if you manage to get five influencers to share, you'll get 400% more shares. This insight alone makes it clear how massive viral videos can get hundreds of millions of views in a very short period when dozens (or even hundreds) of influencers start sharing it.

Although planning a viral post may be a good use of time, it is also important to note that viral content is extremely rare. There are billions of posts made every day across all the major social networks, and yet there are only a handful of viral posts that rise to the top in any given month. Everyone *wants* a viral post, too. So you are competing against everyone else using the same tactics that you have access to. My advice is to plan as if your content can go viral and be patient when it doesn't. When your time comes, as it did for Oreo, you will know what to post. Move fast, be authentic, and once your post has traction, let the social media networks do the work for you.

Before We Continue...

This chapter doesn't have an exercise or assignment on purpose. We are going to make our way through the Campaign Car Wash in its entirety before we start building. So as long as you understand the concepts in this chapter, it's okay to continue. We will pull everything together soon enough.

THE CAMPAIGN CARWASH
PART 2: MEDIUM

Now that you understand the three types of content style, you can start to imagine how those styles will take shape. The form that your content takes is known as its *medium*. Your Big Idea and content style make up your campaign's soul, and your medium makes up your campaign's body. It determines how your campaign looks, sounds, tastes, feels, and smells. A marketer has four primary mediums that can be used to give birth to a campaign:

1. Written
2. Auditory
3. Multimedia
4. Experiential

An important thing to remember as we go through these four categories is that each one gets more complicated as we go. Written and auditory deal with only one sense at a time, Multimedia deals with two (Sound & Sight), and Experiential deals with more than two at a time. The reason we prioritize content medium by the number of senses involved is that the **content production cost** rises as your campaign becomes more sensory-rich.

That doesn't mean that more complicated (or expensive) mediums will automatically work better. As we continue to explore each of these four mediums, you will get a better idea of the cost/benefit tradeoff of Experiential content as well as the utter simplicity of Written content, and how they can both play effective roles in your campaign planning process.

The Most Important Factor

As you read through the four mediums below, you will get a better idea of what form of content is going to be best for you. It will be as much of an emotional decision as it will be a logical one; intuition does play a part here. For example, if a solo founder isn't comfortable in front of a camera, multimedia content won't be the best option (at least immediately) for content creation.

Similarly, if you find yourself drawn to the art of writing and believe you express yourself best through that medium, it's *better* to stick with that form of content despite the sensory advantages of the other three mediums.

You should be comfortable with, and confident in, your (or your company's) ability to create content in the mediums of your choosing. That part is key. Keep this in mind as we move on, and consider which medium strikes you as the most comfortable medium. Don't worry about being pigeonholed by just one medium—we will address that later when we return to your marketing operating system.

WRITTEN CONTENT

Written content is one of the oldest forms of communication. It began with cave drawings about 40,000 years ago and got a modern upgrade about 5,000 years ago as ancient civilizations, to the rescue of forgetful husbands everywhere, figured out how to write things down.

From that moment on, everything from to-do lists to books made it possible to *physically save* ideas and thoughts that would have previously been lost in the void of human forgetfulness. But there was still a problem: people still had to *write things down*. You think Carpal Tunnel Syndrome is an issue today? Try being a scribe in a Medieval court.

That all changed with the invention of the printing press in 1450. Suddenly, education became ubiquitous as the cost of reproducing written content dropped… dare I say… *exponentially.* When the internet came along, the cost of that content dropped even further, solidifying the written word's status as **one of the most widely accessible and efficient forms of communication on planet Earth.**

What do I mean by *efficient?*

I mean that writing is the fastest form of communication. The average human mind can interpret the written word faster than the spoken word. Studies indicate that the average human reads at approximately 250 words per minute while the average conversation speed is about 150 words per minute (according to the National Center for Voice and Speech). You would have to be listening to an auctioneer in order to reach the same speed of interpretation as the average person reading words. Say what you want about listening to your podcast on 2X speed, but our brains are still wired to interpret the written word more efficiently than speech. This is most obvious when we look at the flip side of the 2X-speed podcast listeners—speed readers. People who are skilled at speed reading can interpret the written word, at a high level of proven accuracy, at rates of 450 words per minute, and even up to 700 words per minute with the right training.

Written content is simple, easily accessible, and cheap to produce. But, despite its simplicity, it remains a powerful medium. You don't have to look far to see the proof—the Bible, classic novels, and best-selling books are all evidence that the written word is alive and well and not going anywhere. It is even possible to build an entire business on written content alone.

Andre Chaperon did it. Andre is a copywriter (a really good one, at that). A few years ago, he started a company called Tiny Little Businesses (TLB) to share his expertise with the world. TLB's marketing and educational content is 100% created with written content. You will be hard-pressed to find a video-based lesson from him, much less a course. All of TLB's material, including its training programs, is written. When someone buys one of TLB's courses, they get access to a 30,000+ word membership portal where his students can go to learn. Their flagship product, Autoresponder Madness, has been sold thousands and thousands of times and has received critical acclaim from the marketing industry. All through the written medium.

Seth Godin, who we've seen before in this book, writes a blog almost every single day. Twitter was entirely built on short pieces of written content. The media and PR industry is built on written content. We text, WhatsApp, email, and iMessage our friends and colleagues regularly, often on a minute-to-minute basis.

Written content is woven into the fabric of our culture. The extent to which you use written content is up to you; you can rely on it solely for your website copy or you can do what Andre did with TLB and rely on it exclusively, or you can find a middle ground that is right for you. The important thing is that you go through the thought process of *deciding* whether Written content is right for you and your company's brand—and how heavily you would like to rely on it.

Most Common Forms Of Written Content

Let's make this concrete. The list below contains some common forms of written content that you can use in your campaign. You don't need to write these down. They will be included in a big list that comes later. For now, look through the list and think about what form of written content you feel called to create. Feel free to circle or underline any of them, write in the margins, and add other forms that you would like to leverage through your marketing:

- Blogs
- Books
- News articles

- Written social media posts
- Text messages (including Messenger, iMessage, WhatsApp, SMS, and others)
- Emails
- Website content
- Skywriters & Blimps (yup!)
- App notifications
- Text ads
- Research reports
- Whitepapers
- Workbooks

AUDITORY CONTENT

D r. Matthias Mehl is an Associate Professor in the Department of Psychology at the University of Arizona. In 2014, he conducted a study on the number of words the average person says in a single day, landing at an average of 15,669 words for men and 16,215 for women.

That's a lot of talking.

We learn to speak as children before we learn to read. While the written word is the more efficient form of communication, the spoken word is our longest held. It is also our most celebrated; parents often celebrate their child's first spoken words more than their child's first written word. There is more excitement around the spoken word than the written word. This is at least partially due to the fact that we can pack more emotion into the spoken word than we can with the written word. We can speak one word in many different ways using intonation and inflection to communicate our feelings. This isn't possible in the written word without punctuation, and even then, subtle vocal cues can't be captured. This is why screenplay writing requires annotations and notes to explain *exactly how* a character is feeling.

The spoken word constitutes a large portion of the category we're exploring here: auditory content. What does auditory content look like in the marketing world? Well, any form of content that can be played over a speaker is considered auditory. The most common and popular forms are phone calls, commercials, shows, music, and sonic branding.

Phone calls, including voicemails, are a very traditional form of auditory content. You have likely received countless sales calls and spam callers on your phone. This is for a good reason—we talk over the phone *a lot*. Which means we are used to it and comfortable with it. Over 5 billion people own a mobile phone and, although we spend plenty of time texting and playing Angry Birds, we still spend plenty of time using it to actually talk to people (you know, with our mouths). Due to spam callers and highly aggressive salespeople, phone conversations are a highly abused form of auditory content, but it is still worth noting as a valuable medium. Whenever a high-stakes deal is in the works, or when a Gen X'er wants to talk to someone in person, the phone is the #1 form of communication to use. There is a high level of comfort with using our phones and most people feel better knowing that there is someone on the other line who is totally focused on helping us out. Having that trust built into the very fabric of an auditory medium is helpful for businesses who prioritize one-on-one communication and quality customer service.

Commercials are short bursts of auditory content, usually lasting between 15 and 60 seconds, depending on the spot available. Pretty much everyone has heard a radio or podcast commercial at some point, so I won't belabor this point other than to say the following. The two important pieces to consider when creating a commercial are (1) the content itself and (2) the speaker. The content is important for obvious reasons—what is actually *said*, and in what *order*, makes the difference between a boring commercial and an exciting and valuable one. The speaker is important because the gender, age, and energy level of the person doing the talking all have an effect. AARP commercials are spoken by people in their 50's and older while a commercial for an upcoming pop music concert will have someone in their 20's speaking. A commercial for a women's product will have a female speaker, whereas a commercial for a male product will have a guy. As far as energy levels go, it is important to decide the right energy level for your audience—otherwise the brand feeling will be lost. A radio commercial for a Labor Day sale at your local mattress store will have a high level of energy powerful enough to share the exciting and time-sensitive deals available. On the other hand, a commercial for a local spa will sound relaxed and serene. Two very different energy levels for two very different brands.

Shows, whether hosted over the radio or on a podcast, have the blessing and curse of a single host or a rarely changing group of hosts. The blessing is that the host(s) can build a relationship with the audience which has a cumulative listener effect and helps the show's following grow. The curse is that if the host doesn't have the right energy or doesn't share valuable enough content, the show won't succeed—plus it's hard to replace a host. Radio and podcast shows with a revolving door of hosts will never gain enough traction to build a loyal following. This is one of the reasons why radio shows like Howard Stern and podcasts like the Joe Rogan Experience are built on the personal brand of the host themselves. It is often better to go all-in on the host and capitalize on the more intimate audience connection driven by a personal brand than to have a generic show name that doesn't communicate the host's brand in any way. When you build that brand, though, you build a loyal following of people who listen to your show to be entertained, educated, or inspired.

Music is another form of auditory content. An art form unto itself, music plays a large role in setting a mood, creating shared experiences, and in some cases, enticing action. I won't explore the productized side of music here since, for the musicians reading this, the music *is* the product. What we *will* explore is how to leverage music for the purposes of your campaign.

Adding music to a shopping experience, an app interface, a gamified online course, or another step of your customer journey can have a positive effect on your brand experience. In a two-week study conducted by the University of Leicester, researchers played two types of music in the wine section of a grocery store. During one half of the time, they played French music. During the other half of the time, they played German music. Over the two-week period, when German music was played, the vast majority of shoppers bought German wine. On French music days, the majority bought French wine. The study found that shoppers were substantially more likely to purchase wine associated with the music being played. So, the next time you are in a grocery store buying wine or food, take a moment and listen to the music in the background. It might be influencing what you buy.

Music can also be used to increase product engagement through gamification. The online course platform Xperiencify uses musical sound effects to gamify their clients' courses. Their strategy in using these sounds, which play when someone finishes a task or lesson, is to increase the rate at which their clients' customers finish the course. It is a simple and powerful way of using psychological reward mechanisms to get people more committed to completing a large goal (like finishing a training program).

One of the most popular applications of music to marketing content is combining it with video content. This is a powerful strategy, but it also enters the realm of Multimedia content, which we will explore shortly.

Sonic Branding is the use of sounds and, in some cases, music, to deepen the sensory experience of your brand. It is often used in conjunction with Multimedia and Experiential mediums, but the goal is for your brand's sounds to be powerful enough to be recognized on their own with no other cues. The term used to describe a sonic branding asset is a *sound trademark*.

The legal definition of a sound trademark is relatively vague, but the practical definition is useful. It's basically a modern-day jingle. Some examples of sound trademarks include the Apple Mac startup chime, the MGM lion roar, the NBC three-note chime, the Intel Inside jingle, the McDonald's *I'm lovin' it* jingle, and the orchestral fanfares for DreamWorks Animation and Marvel Studios. These are all sounds or musical pieces that customers can immediately recognize without seeing anything visual.

Creating a sound trademark can make your brand more memorable and recognizable. It can also be applied to anything; Apple didn't *have to* code their computers to play the startup chime, but they chose to. Rumor is that Steve Jobs, being a big fan of the Beatles, based that sound on the F-sharp chord that plays at the end of *Sergeant Pepper's Lonely Hearts Club Band*. Regardless, when you hear that chime, you immediately know it's a Mac. Good old Steve (rest in peace).

Sonic branding can have a place in any business—and in any place within the product experience. The value of a sound trademark is bigger than can be stuffed into just one marketing initiative. In the context of your campaign, you may want to consider taking any sonic trademark you create and adding it to the overall product experience (and not confined within the boundaries of just one campaign).

Most Common Forms of Auditory Content

Consider the various forms of auditory content listed below. Which ones suit your brand best? Which ones stick out to you as contenders for the campaign you are working on now? Think about this—and we will return to the full list in the next exercise.

- Live phone call
- Robotic phone call (be careful with this)
- Voicemail drops
- Podcast show
- Podcast commercial
- Radio show
- Radio commercial

MULTIMEDIA CONTENT

They say a picture is worth a thousand words.

When I was in sixth grade, I decided to put that theory to the test with a 1,000-word essay I was assigned to write. So I turned in a piece of paper printed with a single photo and the phrase *"1,000 words"* printed underneath.

My teacher didn't think it was that funny, but at least I got a little street cred with my friends.

It took my failed experiment and a few years, but I came to learn that pictures *can be* worth a thousand words—but only when used properly. In the right context, they can communicate more than words. While the spoken word (and auditory content in general) can evoke emotion over the course of a conversation, episode, track, or sound clip, pictures and videos can evoke an *even more intense* emotional response in a matter of *seconds*. Seeing something with your own eyes can cut through the inefficiencies of letting your audience's imagination do all the work and, as a result, it can end up being a more immersive experience.

Multimedia content is created when we enter the visual realm beyond the written and verbal word. Put into practice, Multimedia content takes two forms: photos and videos.

Photos

Photography forms the visual foundation of websites, magazines, newspapers, direct mailers, and emails. David Ogilvy is famous for using his ⅔ layout in print ads. He prioritized the image above the copywriting, letting the image capture the reader's attention and then allowing them to move on to the written word in order to learn more. Ogilvy tested this layout extensively and explained in *Ogilvy On Advertising* that advertising either suffers from *Artdirectoritis* (over-designing) or the advertisers themselves relying too much on making ads that *look like ads*, which end up having "inherited graphic conventions which telegraph to the reader, 'This is only an advertisement. *Skip it.'"*

Ogilvy was right. Pictures can be used too much, and they can also be used too little. They can be overproduced, and they can also be under-integrated. These days, we have tools that allow us to test what photos work best in certain places, but that also doesn't change the fact that you *must* be thoughtful about which photos you choose and how you use them. They will have a potent effect on your content, and that effect can be equally positive or negative. Great photographers are great for a reason.

Pictures, although powerful, are also limited. A great photo may tell more than half the story, but it still needs words to clarify the message.

It takes Written or Auditory content to fill in the blanks of a photo. When you see a billboard for a local injury attorney, just having the person's picture on the billboard explains nothing—it's just a guy or gal smiling at you. There *must* be some text added to the billboard for you to know exactly what's being explained. Only with a *huuuuge* level of brand recognition can you do an image-only ad. A magazine ad with a basketball player and the Nike swoosh in the corner is obviously a Nike ad—there doesn't need to be a text overlay. But even then, Nike would be running a branding campaign, not a direct response campaign. If they were running a special promotion or announcing a new type of sneaker, nobody would know. Even Apple does this in their iPhone ads; you may even recognize the newest model iPhone on a billboard, but Apple still puts *iPhone 12* (or whatever is the latest model) in the corner so people know it is new.

Video

The second and more popular form of Multimedia content is video. Video content production has skyrocketed in popularity over the last few years as internet bandwidth has increased and social media platforms have learned that users spend more time looking at their feeds when they have videos to watch.

Videos engage us visually and auditorily—together, those two senses have the power to keep us firmly seated in a movie theater or our office chairs for hours on end. When used effectively, video content can build a memorable and positive brand relationship with your audience. And the best part is that there are new types of video assets coming into the market every day, from TikTok to Facebook Live. Of course, this contributes to the micro-niching problem we reviewed earlier in this book. But fear not—we will be addressing the right ones for you soon enough.

A lot of times, companies get overwhelmed by the cost of producing high quality video content. This is another misleading trend; in many cases, videos that are simply recorded from a phone and posted to social media perform better than their highly edited and professionally branded versions. This is because we, as a population, are used to seeing ugly, blurry videos from our friends and family. We've gotten used to the "instant" nature of the content shared by the people we love. So, when you watch an "instant" video from an influencer, like when you watch a celebrity's Instagram Story, you feel like you are closer to them. You have an insider's look at their daily life, which makes you feel more connected to them. So don't shy away from raw, unedited content in your campaign; in many cases, it is the best type of content you can create.

Most Common Forms of Multimedia Content

I have separated this list into two categories (Pictures and Videos) to make it easier to differentiate. Take a look and consider which forms of Multimedia content could serve your campaign best. We will come back to these in the exercise. Here are some examples of how **photos** can be used in your campaign:

- Magazine & newspaper ads
- Billboards
- Bus stop and subway posters
- Bus & truck wraps
- Stickers
- User-generated social content
- Flyers

And here are some examples of how **video** can be used in your campaign:

- Traditional (landscape format under 10 minutes)
- Stories (short bursts of vertical video)
- Social media video ads (in both of the above formats)
- Shorts (short bursts of landscape video)
- Reels (short video clips glued together or matched with music clips)
- Live streams
- Video messaging
- Webinars
- Video series (3 or more videos over 10 minutes each)
- Masterclasses (on-demand videos over 45 minutes)

- Commercials (including TV and streaming services like Hulu and You-Tube)
- Video podcasts
- Video conferences/meetings
- Virtual summits

EXPERIENTIAL CONTENT

E xperiential content is the final style we will explore. This style of marketing is different from the others because it focuses on creating a brand experience that goes beyond the auditory and visual realms and spreads across three or more senses.

In-person events are the first and most accessible form of Experiential content. Speaking gigs, in particular, are a great way to get your brand and message in front of a live audience. You can use the energy of an in-person event to connect with a large group of people who are there to listen to *you*. They have committed time, whether that is a few minutes or a few hours or even multiple days, to experience your brand. You can write a talk, take part in a panel discussion, design a group workshop, or even host a dinner—it all falls under the category of Experiential content. No matter the label you give it, if you are the person at the front of the room who everyone else is listening to, you are creating Experiential content.

When appearing at an in-person event, it is important to consider how you appear, how you speak, the aesthetics of the room, the comfort of your audience's chairs, and all kinds of other sensory inputs in play when you are running the show. Tony Robbins is famous in the marketing world for designing his events at such a deep level of detail that it feels like no stone was unturned. His team controls the temperature of the room, the brightness of the lights, the volume and style of the music, and all kinds of other Experiential factors in order to create the ultimate immersive experience.

Now, if you are a keynote speaker, odds are that you won't have control over those kinds of event details. You only get to do that if you are the host. But in any case, when you are the speaker, the room is yours. You have the full attention of your audience, which means the way you look, the way you carry yourself, the way you speak, and your presentation's content all play a large role in the experience you're creating.

Another great example of experiential marketing is a **multi-sensory experience**. I like to explain this category by starting with how scents are used in marketing (known as *Olfactory marketing*).

If you've ever walked into a Subway, you know what it smells like. There is a unique scent to Subway stores that doesn't exist in any other store. You also might know the signature smell of Abercrombie & Fitch, Burger King, a new car, or Cinnabon. All these brands use carefully engineered scents that, over time, become identifiable by customers as "the way the brand smells." Some companies use nebulizers or aerosol sprays to create a uniform scent in whatever location or product they control.

There is a scientific reason for this. From casinos to grocery stores to hotel lobbies, specific scents are added to encourage purchasing or brand engagement. For example, the smell of lemon has been proven to increase the desire to clean your house.

When you coordinate that scent with the right imagery and audio, our brains are overloaded with the desire to engage further. Neuromarketing specialist Martin Lindstrom calls this the "sensory assault," and he is not wrong. If you visit a Disney theme park, you will walk by bushes and trees with scent machines that release the smell of cotton candy, caramel apple, and popcorn. Since smell accounts for 80% of our sense of taste, it is not hard to understand why scent machines are used so ubiquitously—yet we often don't know it. Many of these scents are released in such low quantities that, at times, it is only noticeable on a subconscious level. And when we do know it, unless you've read this book or are an expert familiar with olfactory marketing, you would walk through Disney World assuming it was just the smell emanating from the cotton candy stand that was *conveniently* placed in your line of sight when you smelled that sweet sugary scent.

While the use of scents is a powerful form of Experiential marketing, it is not nearly as powerful on its own. When paired with other senses and other marketing channels, you can create a carefully branded experience that is unique to your company. This is what I mean by a "multisensory experience."

There are two factors that contribute to the success of a multisensory experience. The first is relatively obvious, **multi-sensory engagement,** and the second is less obvious: **cumulative exposure.**

Multi-sensory Engagement

Multi-sensory engagement occurs when you experience what Lindstrom mentioned above as a sensory assault. Let's take your local Cinnabon as an example.

When you walk by a Cinnabon store, even if you don't see the sign, you smell it (Sense: Smell). Once you smell it, you start looking for it and see the sign (Sense: Sight). By then, you will know the brand—the look and feel of the Cinnabon logo, the sight of the warm buns sitting under the heat lamps, and the wide-open doorway inviting you to enter. By now, you may be thinking of a Cinnabon you once tasted (and if you are not doing it consciously, your subconscious mind is doing it for you). By now, the memory of eating a cinnamon bun and the smell of fresh Cinnabons have already made your mouth water. Now your brain wants to check the box of a third sense: taste.

Just using two senses, Cinnabon creates an almost irresistible urge to check off that third box: tasting a cinnamon bun. And once you end up buying one, you automatically engage the fourth sense, Touch. The texture of the bun itself in your hand and in your mouth, the texture of the icing as your teeth bite down, and the texture of the bread as you chew it are all part of the brand experience (and all are engineered to be as pleasant and addictive as possible). So far, Cinnabon has engaged at least four of the five senses: Sight, Smell, Taste, and Touch. If you're wondering what they do to engage Sound in the brand experience, all you have to do is visit a local Cinnabon to listen to the sounds in the store itself, from the soundtrack to the sound of fresh buns being dropped into the heated display case. Some of these sounds are inherent in the business itself and others are carefully thought out.

If you don't have a physical store, you might be wondering how Experiential content fits into a digital marketing strategy. This is where cutting-edge technology like Virtual Reality and Augmented Reality come into play. The rise of these technologies in recent years has begun to reap benefits for companies that use it. Load up one of Apple's web pages for a MacBook or iPhone and you'll find a fully immersive Augmented Reality experience that lets you view a new iPhone model in the palm of your hand. Snapchat, Facebook, and TikTok all have Augmented Reality filters in their apps that allow you to see a 3D image right in front of you just by activating your phone's camera. Companies are already integrating this technology into their campaigns. You can even buy haptic devices to add "feeling" to videogames. All of this exists today.

Cumulative Experiences

Another form of multi-sensory experiences is engaging with people across different channels—I call this *cumulative exposure*.

In 2016, Snickers partnered with 7-Eleven to promote a new campaign they called the *Hungerithm*. By using a computer algorithm developed by MIT, Snickers was able to measure and publish the online "mood" by reading the level of anger and sarcasm in Twitter posts across the internet. It then assigned an anger "score" to the internet and posted it in a live dashboard on the *Hungerithm* website. As the internet grew angrier, the cost of a Snickers bar at your local 7Eleven store went down. This fed a massive level of brand exposure for Snickers and 7Eleven. The way they blurred the lines between the real world and the digital world was compelling and creative, and Snickers lovers everywhere thought so, too. The 7Eleven and Snickers campaign built *cumulative exposure* into their campaign, and those repeated campaign exposures added up to create something bigger and more successful than a normal campaign would be able to achieve.

First, there was an additive experience created when customers saw the campaign take shape in both the digital and physical worlds (the *Hungerithm* website and the physical 7Eleven store). This served to increase the campaign's exposure as well as the tangibility of the campaign. In other words, consumers could literally get their hands on a popular trend by buying a Snickers bar at an all-time low price. There was also a campaign journey that built up over the process of (1) making a social media post, (2) seeing the effect on the *Hungerithm* site (known as a Feedback Loop), and then (3) walking into the local 7Eleven store to buy a Snickers bar.

There was also a cumulative *brand* experience that built up by adding together the brand equity of Snickers and 7Eleven. Together, their combined reputation, authenticity, and authority in the market created a highly trustworthy and engaging campaign that they wouldn't have been able to achieve by themselves. This is the power of *cumulative exposure* in a multi-sensory Experiential campaign. You can leverage all kinds of campaign elements to build a cumulative experience: unexpected steps in the customer journey, multiple brand experiences, user-generated content, rewards, PR stunts, celebrity endorsements, personalized messaging, physical and digital integration, and more.

Most Common Forms of Experiential Content

Although Experiential content takes many, many forms in the real world, I've put a list of examples below for you to consider. Regardless of whether your business is digital or has a brick-and-mortar location, consider each of these options carefully.

- Conference booth experiences
- Retail shopping experiences
- Concerts
- Intra-industry partnerships
- Speaking gigs
- Interactive workshops
- Gifts
- Competitions/Challenges/Contests
- Referral Networks
- Shippable at-home workshop/webinar kits
- Unique product packaging

THE CAMPAIGN CAR WASH
PART 3: THE EXPOSURE

Welcome to the final stage of the Campaign Car Wash! It's time for the rubber to meet the road. By now, you have a Big Idea to pursue—that will be the beating heart of your campaign. You have your minimum viable audience or secondary audience, which means you know the exact group of people you'll be reaching with your campaign. You are also familiar with the type of content style and medium you are most excited to create. Now it is time to figure out how you are going to get that content out to the world.

Before I continue, a word of praise: **well done.** The next few chapters contain the steps that most people *start* with. It is the place where micro-niches reign and consultants, agencies, and software platforms try to focus your attention before you have gone through the hard bit and figured out what your campaign is actually "about." Now that you know, though, you are entering the micro-niche arena with your head on straight, ready to tackle whatever is thrown at you. You are going to be able to make more intelligent choices with the tools you use and the consultants you choose to hire. In short, you are quickly becoming a Marketing Scientist. Give yourself a pat on the back—and let's get started.

Exposure, the final step of the Campaign Car Wash, is the process of getting your audience's attention. This means we must figure out where your audience is—where they are spending their time. Sure, it could be Facebook, but it could also be the local yoga studio. Or an industry conference. Or any number of other places. Getting exposure is about picking the right locations to share your campaign's content so it gets maximum attention from the right people. In marketing, we call these locations **channels.** Whenever you see me use that word, I'm describing one *specific location*, whether online or offline, that you can share your content with your audience.

WHAT IS ATTRIBUTION?

By far and away, the biggest challenge when dealing with marketing channels is knowing how to track their success. The process used to track a channel's marketing performance is known as *attribution*. Attribution is a feature of every analytics platform out there. It is focused on doing one thing very well: tracing a customer's purchase back to the channel that initially grabbed their attention[9].

Attribution is a complicated process and typically requires digital marketing technology in order to work. You can attribute offline purchases to certain channels, but it's cumbersome—it's kind of like when a local doctor asks you where you found out about them. It's possible, but not very scalable. That means, on a practical level, that the only high-volume channels that can be accurately traced to a customer's purchase are in the digital realm, like social media and email. We call these **attributed channels**. Any channels that can't be digitally traced back to a purchase are called **unattributed channels.**

Let's say you rent a billboard positioned next to a local highway. The billboard is nicely designed, has all the right messaging, and tells people to call your phone number. Over the following two weeks, your business gets a couple dozen phone calls from people wanting to buy your product. You make some sales, things look peachy, and then your marketing meeting arrives, and you sit down to evaluate the ROI of your billboard investment. How do you figure out which phone calls originated from the billboard versus from other unpaid sources like Google search and referrals?

The answer is *you can't*. Same thing goes for TV ads, posters, and direct mailers. These are unattributed channels, and although they *can* add a high level

---

9   In technical marketing terms, this is called *first-click attribution*. There's a whole field called attribution modeling which explores the various ways you can give credit to channels that played a part in attracting new customers. This is an advanced field beyond the scope of this book, but worth investigating if you begin to use more than just a handful of channels in your marketing.

of sales to your business, they are not able to be technologically traced back to transactions. From a strictly logical perspective, this makes unattributed channels a riskier investment than attributed channels.

Now, there *are* ways to build some traceability into some unattributed channels. This is called **manual attribution.** You can have tracking phone numbers that are used exclusively in your billboard ads. You can use "short links" in your direct mailers that send people to a web page exclusively for direct mail recipients. When all else fails, you can ask the customer how they found out about you. But manual attribution methods are slightly flawed in that they introduce the possibility of errors into your tracking. Someone who saw the billboard could share the phone number with a friend (leading to a referral being mislabeled as a billboard-driven customer). A direct mail recipient could decide to just go to your home page instead of the short link you gave them (leading to a direct mail recipient being mislabeled as a direct traffic visitor on your website).

These are all flaws inherent in manual attribution. But that doesn't mean the benefits don't outweigh the risks. If you get 100 customers from a billboard ad and a small handful of those customers were miscategorized, it's not the end of the world. But it *is* an entry-point for dirty data into your analytics, so be careful how many corners you cut in this arena. Too many of these dirty data entry-points will lead to misleading reports and bad decisions.

Attributed channels, on the other hand, have none of these downsides. Since they are built in the digital realm, they have built-in tracking. When you are dealing with digital channels, you have cookies, UTM parameters, and all kinds of other technical stuff *working for you*. Analytics platforms like Oribi, Google Analytics, and Facebook Analytics pull all the data together to tell you very specifically where your customers are coming from.

Let's say I decided to use Facebook as a channel for an upcoming marketing campaign. I would make a few posts on my Facebook page and provide a link back to my website. As people click from any of those posts, my website can see that they're coming from Facebook—and it saves that information to their profile for me to review later. As those people browse my website, I can see what pages they view—that's saved to their profile, too. And when they make a purchase, something called an "event" is added to my new customer's profile. That means I can go look at a list of all the events across my entire website and see how many people bought after clicking on one of my Facebook posts. I can also see what pages my Facebook visitors view the most and what products they are likely to buy. With enough data, I can determine how my Facebook posts perform against each other as well as how they perform compared to other channels—which allows me to determine whether to invest further in one channel or another. This is all possible because of attribution. You would not be able to see any of that data with a billboard ad or a TV commercial.

Now that you understand the principles of attribution, it is now possible to look at your channels with a clear understanding of their pros and cons. I find it useful to organize channels into a few categories: Owned Channels, Paid Channels, and Earned Channels. Each of these categories contains methods of getting your campaign content out into the world.

OWNED CHANNELS

Owned Channels are communication methods that you control, such as email. You own your email list, you control the look and feel of the email templates, and you decide what content is inside the emails themselves. Owned channels give you direct lines of communication with your audience and allow you to build long-term relationships without relying on anyone else to get the word out for you. They also have the highest longevity out of the three types of channels. For example, you control your blog, which means you control how long any given blog post is published on your website. This isn't true for Paid Channels, where your content disappears when you stop investing in ads. It is also not true of Earned Channels, where another company or person controls how long your content is published (Huffington Post, for example, can delete a post featuring your business, and they can do so at any time they please).

An important distinction to consider with Owned Channels is whether a channel is inbound or outbound. The difference lies in whether you attracted your customer through the channel, or they sought you out through that channel. **Inbound** channels are initiated by the customer while **outbound** channels are initiated by you. One is not better than the other—for example, blog posts create inbound traffic by ranking highly in search results and cold calling (an outbound method) is still a legitimate sales strategy.

Practically speaking, however, outbound email, phone calls, and messages are superior to their inbound counterparts. You know where those emails or phone numbers came from and thus can increase or decrease your investment in email or phone number collection efforts. That is not possible with inbound email or phone channels—you can't measure where people are getting your phone number or email address from since it is likely listed in all kinds of places (which makes it difficult to improve the performance of that channel). For this reason, I've left inbound email and phone off the list of owned channels below. Here are some examples of Owned Channels:

- Outbound Email
- Outbound Phone Calls
- Outbound Messages (SMS and others)
- Blogs (RSS Feed)
- Website/Funnel
- Facebook Group
- Mobile App
- Joint Venture/Affiliate Initiatives
- Podcasts
- Radio Shows
- Social Media Posts[10]
- Hosted Event
- Hosted Webinar
- Retail Location
- Referral Networks (Word of Mouth)

Expanding On The Inbound/Outbound Debate

A practical way to think about the difference between inbound and outbound channels is a business that relies solely on getting referrals. That would mean they are reliant exclusively on *inbound* email, phone calls, and messages from people who were referred to them.

This is a risky business model that has a low probability of growth. Referral-only businesses don't have much control over the *flow* of their inbound referrals. Their only choice is to switch their focus to outbound emails, phone calls, and messages. That would take the form of a referral campaign that uses outbound channels targeted at existing customers who are likely to give referrals. See how the strategy switches from something that can't be controlled to something that *can* be controlled? Instead of waiting for calls to come in (inbound), you must go out and get them (outbound).

---

10 I'm including this and Facebook Groups as owned content since you control the posts themselves, but always keep in mind that you can have a social media profile shut down at any time. Facebook famously went down for a few hours in October 2021 and served as a grim reminder to everyone whose livelihood depended on their organic Facebook traffic. Never put all your eggs in someone else's basket! This is as true for organic traffic as it is for a TikTok profile.

℘ PAID CHANNELS

Paid Channels are methods of reaching your audience through advertisements and other paid placements like sponsorships. The single greatest advantage of using paid channels is scalability. You can increase and decrease your ad budget very quickly, which means when a channel is working well, you can put more money into it immediately and see immediate results.

Depending on your business model, one drawback of Paid Channels is that you have less control over what you can and cannot promote. Ad platforms like Facebook and Google have strict rules around what you can say and show its users. There are two types of rules: **Prohibited Content** and **Restricted Content.**

Prohibited Content rules state that you can't advertise certain types of material. This is to enforce legality as well as a safe and comfortable experience for the people seeing the ads. Each ad network has their own Prohibited Content policies, but they are typically the same no matter where you are advertising. For example, this is Facebook's current list of Prohibited Content:

- Illegal Products or Services
- Discriminatory Practices
- Tobacco and Related Products
- Unsafe Substances
- Weapons, Ammunition, or Explosives
- Adult Products or Services
- Adult Content
- Third-Party Infringement[11]
- Sensational Content

---

11   You can't run ads that infringe on another company or person's rights, such as using another company's logo without permission.

- Personal Attributes[12]
- Misinformation[13]
- Controversial Content[14]
- Non-Functional Landing Page
- Cheating and Deceitful Practices
- Grammar & Profanity
- Nonexistent Functionality
- Personal Health[15]
- Payday Loans, Paycheck Advances, and Bail Bonds
- Multilevel Marketing
- Penny Auctions
- Misleading Claims
- Low Quality or Disruptive Content
- Spyware or Malware
- Unacceptable Business Practices[16]
- Circumventing Systems[17]
- Prohibited Financial Products and Services
- Sale of Body Parts[18]
- Vaccine Discouragement

For most businesses, these rules don't pose a threat, but it is important that you know that they are there so you don't step on any landmines.

Restricted Content is a type of ad content that's not banned entirely (as with Prohibited Content) but *is* monitored closely by the ad networks. If you are in a highly regulated industry, you will probably fit into a Restricted Content category. This doesn't mean that you can't run ads, but it does mean that the

---

12 Facebook will take down your ad if you mention personal attributes, like trying to make an assertion of the ad reader's race, sexual orientation, or religion.

13 This prohibition has been enforced a lot in recent years. Facebook has a team of fact-checkers that will double-check any claims or assertions you make in your ad.

14 This is a very general label, but this prohibition basically means that you can't, in Facebook's words, "exploit crises or controversial political or social issues for commercial purposes."

15 Specifically, you can't include before-and-after pictures of people or promote content that sets unrealistic expectations for health-related results from your product, including any assertions that may create a sense of negative self-image.

16 Basically, don't be a scam artist.

17 Facebook checks whether your ad is trying to find a loophole or creative solution around their ad policies

18 This is a relatively new one. I guess it was a problem at some point...

ad network will hold you accountable to the advertising standards set by your industry, or even standards they have set themselves in order to protect their customers' experience. Here is Facebook's current list of Restricted Content:

- Alcohol
- Dating
- Online Gambling & Gaming
- Promotion of Online Pharmacies
- Promotion of Over-The-Counter Drugs
- Subscription Services[19]
- Financial and Insurance Products and Services
- Branded Content[20]
- Ads About Social Issues, Elections, or Politics[21]
- Disclaimers About Social Issues, Elections, or Politics
- Cryptocurrency Products and Services
- Drug and Alcohol Addiction Treatment
- Cosmetic Procedures and Wellness[22]
- Social Casino Games
- Promotion of Prescription Drugs

In some cases, you will have to submit an application with the ad network to run ads in any of these categories. Once again, this is not a ban—it is just the ad network covering their bases to make sure that their customers are seeing ads from reputable companies with all the right licensing and registrations to run promotions.

With these policies in mind, we can now explore what types of Paid Channels you can pursue to get your campaign content in front of a larger audience than you would be able to reach with Owned Channels and Earned Channels alone.

There are a lot of Paid Channels you can choose from. These days, Facebook and Google are the most popular digital ad options, but it would be a mistake to think they are the only ones at your disposal. Micro-niche mayhem can force

---

19   If you run a subscription business, don't be intimidated. This is just Facebook saying they have the authority to shut down ads for subscription services that are impossible to cancel or otherwise try to "trick" customers into paying for a subscription they didn't want.
20   If you are selling a product that is under a different brand than your own, you have to say so and link to the brand.
21   Facebook closely monitors any political ads for accuracy and adherence to local laws and regulations
22   Any ads in this category have to be targeted to people 18 years of age and older

our attention away from more creative (and potentially more profitable) Paid Channels. The way I like to maintain perspective is by isolating the popular digital advertising channels (like Facebook) into their own category, which makes it easier to see the full advertising playing field. I have done that for you below by using three categories.

Digital Networks are platforms that allow you to buy ads for placement on the platform's website (like Facebook) or for placement on a syndicated group of websites that display that platform's ads on their blog or other web pages (like Google Display Network).

Sponsorships allow you to pay another company (one that is *not* an ad platform) to promote your campaign content to their audience.

In-Person Events are methods of reaching audiences through stage-based experiences that other companies are hosting.

Like Digital Networks, the pricing for both Sponsorships and In-Person Events are determined by the company you are paying for the exposure. In some cases, such as a conference booth, there is a flat fee. In other cases, such as an affiliate partnership, there is a commission structure in place. These pricing structures are chosen by the host company and can vary.

Let's explore some examples of Paid Channels below. Keep in mind that this is **not** an exhaustive list. As you know, new platforms are popping up all the time, as are new types of events and sponsorships. You can use this list as a launching pad for your next campaign. When the time comes to plan another one, you can use the upcoming exercise as a forum to discuss and evaluate all the new and exciting channels that have entered the market. Here are some examples of Paid Channels:

Digital Networks
- Facebook
- Instagram[23]
- Google

---

23 Facebook owns Instagram and thus integrates Instagram ads into the Facebook Ads Manager. I am including Instagram as its own channel here because users engage with Instagram in an isolated environment (the Instagram app) and, more importantly, behave differently and have different buying patterns than they have in the Facebook ecosystem.

- YouTube[24]
- TikTok
- Pinterest
- Snapchat Ads
- Spotify Ads
- Amazon
- Apple App Store
- Yahoo!
- Bing
- Chumbox Ads (Taboola, Outbrain, Teads, and Nativo[25])

Sponsorships

- Event Sponsorships
- Virtual Summit Sponsorships
- Non-Profit Sponsorships
- Affiliate Partnerships
- Externally Hosted Webinars
- Podcast Sponsorships
- Radio Commercials

In-Person Events

- Conference Booths
- Pay-To-Speak Gigs
- Pay-To-Host Workshop
- Market Booths[26]

You may notice that events (like webinars and conferences) are on this list along with the Owned Channels list. This is purposeful. An event hosted by

---

24 Google owns YouTube, but YouTube is a platform dedicated solely to video whereas traditional Google ads are not. As I mentioned in the footnote above, people behave differently on YouTube than they do when searching on Google. That is why YouTube is in a category of its own.

25 These four are also known as *Native Ad Platforms*. They give you the ability, like Google does, to display your ads on websites across the internet. They are usually used to fill the *recommended articles* sections of editorial websites like USA Today, Business Insider, and Fox.

26 Examples of Market Booths include buying space at a farmer's market, setting up a stand outside a local business, and having sales reps walking around a busy concourse.

someone else is your method of exposure—whereas a self-hosted event can also be a channel, but it also requires you to fill the room. This is an important distinction that forms the boundaries between Owned and Paid events.

Here's a way of thinking about whether to pay for a sponsorship or host your own event. When you pay to speak at an event, you are essentially paying the host to fill the room. You are buying the attention of their audience. If you are hosting your own event, regardless of whether it is digital or in-person, you've already paid to fill the room. The audience already knows who you are by the time they're in the room—that leads to higher conversion rates, but those conversions are also more expensive. This is why companies like ClickFunnels pay to sponsor hundreds of conferences and events per year while they only host one conference themselves. It costs *way* more to host an event than it does to sponsor one, and you get almost the same level of audience exposure. ClickFunnels pays a small fraction of the amount of their annual conference to sponsor an event, but they are still reaching a large audience. With enough volume of sponsorships, they can get many times the number of sales they would have received from their annual event—just from sponsorships.

When deciding which Paid Channel is best for you, do your research. Specifically, you want to consider the **audience characteristics** of that particular channel.

The audience characteristics of each channel in the list above vary widely. For example, over 77% of Pinterest users are female, Instagram and Snapchat are primarily used by people between the ages of 18 and 24, and most LinkedIn users earn over $75,000 per year. These are all stats available with a quick Google search. Just type in *[CHANNEL NAME] audience demographics* and you can learn everything you need to know. For workshops, conferences, and speaking gigs, try to get audience characteristic information from the event host. If the host has a sponsorship page for their event, these stats are often published. *Use this data for your decision-making.* If there is a company hosting a popular industry event that attracts your ideal audience, becoming a sponsor may be a better investment than hosting your own event or running an ad campaign.

ℰ EARNED CHANNELS

Earned channels include any form of exposure that has been given to you as a result of PR (public relations) efforts, partnerships, or joint ventures. These are all unpaid, although in some cases like a Joint Venture Speaking Gig, profit-sharing agreements can be put in place on the "back-end" of the channel. This means that if you are invited to speak at an external event (one you are not hosting) without any investment, there may be an agreement in place with the host to split any sales that occur as a result of the content you share. Here are some examples:

- News Articles
- External Case Studies
- Ratings & Reviews
- TV Appearances
- Ratings & Reviews
- Video Blog Feature
- Documentary Feature
- Appsumo Feature
- Product Hunt Feature
- Joint Venture Speaking Gig
- Joint Venture Virtual Event[27]
- Third-Party Podcast Interviews
- Third-Party Livestream Interviews
- Third-Party Clubhouse Room

The power of Earned Channels lies in something called *borrowed authority.* This is a marketing concept that states if two brands are positioned side-by-side, the lesser-known brand will benefit from the more well-known brand's author-

---

27 This includes webinars, webinar series, virtual summits, masterclasses, and any other virtual event hosted by another company.

ity. This is also known as the "Halo Effect." By being featured on a large news website, for example, you not only benefit from the exposure that the news site generates for you, but you also receive a substantial boost in reputation from being associated with the news company's brand.

When deciding which Earned Channels to use for your campaign, the most important factor to consider is how "high" you'd like to shoot in terms of receiving earned media from another company. For example, it would be relatively difficult to get featured on CNN's website or be invited to talk on *Good Morning America* without having a track record of high-level media coverage. If you don't have such a track record, start with reputable influencers and organizations in your industry who are creating a constant stream of content. This could be your local Rotary club, an industry association, or a popular influencer. You can also hire a publicist to help fast-track the process.

An important thing to remember about Earned Channels is that there is a cumulative effect of each piece of content you "earn." As you are interviewed and featured more often, you and/or your company become more appealing to larger outlets. As that happens, it will become easier to get a spot on a big podcast or TV show. There is momentum to these stories, though, and that momentum gets more important the higher you go in terms of reputability. For example, MSNBC will pay much closer attention to a story that has already been picked up by a few smaller (but still highly reputable) news outlets than it will to a story that had the same number of articles written about it several months ago (in their eyes, it would be "old news").

Summary Of Channels By Medium

I've placed a table below containing a reference for each of the channels we've reviewed above. They are categorized by Medium and type of Exposure. All the channels reviewed over the past several chapters are included in this table, so you don't have to go back and reference past pages if you don't want to. This can be your guide:

	Paid	Earned	Owned
Written	Paid Articles Paid Endorsements Google Search Network	News Articles External Case Studies Ratings & Reviews	Outbound Email Outbound Messages Blogs (RSS Feed) Direct Mail
Auditory	Spotify Ads Pandora Ads Podcast Sponsorship Radio Commercial	Third-Party Podcast Interview Third-Party Clubhouse Room	Podcast Radio Show
Multimedia	Facebook Ads Google Display Network Yahoo Ads Bing Ads YouTube Ads Instagram Ads TikTok Ads Pinterest Ads Snapchat Ads Amazon Ads App Store Ads Chumbox Ads Virtual Summit Sponsorships Non-Profit Sponsorships External Webinars	TV Appearances Video Blog Feature Documentary Feature Third-Party Livestream Interview Appsumo Feature Product Hunt Feature	Social Media Posts Mobile App JV/Affiliate Initiatives Hosted Webinar Website/Funnel Facebook Group Social Media Livestreaming LinkedIn Event Facebook Group
Experiential	Event Sponsorships Conference Booths Pay-To-Speak Gigs Pay-To-Host Workshops Market Booths	JV Speaking Gig JV Virtual Event Speaking Gig	Hosted Event Retail Location Referral Networks (WOM)

For an up-to-date table of channels, visit **heydanrussell.com/snakeoil**

THE CAMPAIGN BRIEFING

Every marketing campaign you create in the Campaign Car Wash should ask your audience to perform a **Call To Action (CTA).** This is the step they need to take to enter the first step of your sales funnel (which we'll get to shortly).

There's a wide array of possible calls to action, from visiting a web page to filling out a form on a clipboard. The important thing to keep in mind is that your audience will not be immediately open to performing "intense" calls to action right out of the gate. For example, sending a text message is less intense than making a phone call. Clicking a link in an email is easier than replying to the email.

Think about what CTA you'd like to use in your campaign. If you already have a sales funnel in place, your CTA should direct people to the first funnel step, whether through a click, a text message, a phone call, or something else. In the exercise that follows, you'll assemble your first campaign, which includes the step of assigning a CTA to each channel to ensure you're requesting the appropriate action, such as a link click for an email broadcast.

Exercise: The Campaign Briefing

It is now time to bring it all together. You have finished the final lesson in the Campaign Car Wash and are now ready to plan your first campaign. To do that, you are going to need to create something called a Campaign Briefing. This is the next piece of your marketing operating system.

A Campaign Briefing is a single document that helps you plan your campaign from top to bottom. It is a place to organize your Big Idea and your channels into a project-management-friendly document. By the time you complete it, you will have the foundations for a well-thought-out marketing campaign positioned for success.

Head over to **heydanrussell.com/snakeoil** to get the Campaign Briefing worksheet.

Assignment: Schedule Your Campaign Creation Meeting

Putting together your Campaign Briefing isn't a one-time process. That's why your marketing operating system needs to have a way to regularly plan new campaigns. The tool we use to do that is called the Campaign Creation Meeting (CCM). This is a 2-hour meeting (or if you are a solo founder, a spot on your calendar) dedicated solely to the creation of a Campaign Briefing. This meeting also includes a 60-minute Big Idea Brainstorm (BIB) to set the right foundation for your campaign's messaging.

To get a downloadable agenda for your Campaign Creation Meeting, head to **heydanrussell.com/snakeoil**

Each CCM should be scheduled at least three months in advance of a campaign's launch. This scheduling gives you enough time to create the necessary content and put campaign infrastructure in place without feeling rushed or skipping important quality assurance steps. Your business's revenue cycles will determine how often these CCMs are held. Read below to find out at what frequency you should host CCMs in your own business. These are suggestions based on the fact that you'll be installing your marketing operating system for the first time, which means that you can customize it to your liking in the future. Want a CCM every month? Great! But at least *start* with the schedules below so you don't get overloaded.

Businesses Without Cycles Or Seasons

If your business doesn't have revenue cycles based on industry trends or seasons, you should host a CCM every three months. This means that you'll launch a new campaign every three months (AKA quarterly). The first CCM you host will plan for a campaign with a launch date three months in advance—so if you are hosting your first CCM in January, your first campaign will launch in April.

You also have the option of scheduling "periodic" CCMs for holidays and important promotional periods like Black Friday. If you would like to do this, you can. But schedule these CCMs only *after* you have placed the first four CCMs on your calendar. Even if periods like Black Friday or Christmas are your biggest sales periods, I urge you to prioritize the quarterly CCMs in order to maintain sustainable marketing operations over the rest of the year.

Cyclical Businesses

If you are a cyclical business, you have two or more revenue cycles per year that aren't driven by the seasons (if you are a seasonal business, skip this and move to the next section). In this case, you should host a CCM three months before each revenue cycle begins.

If your revenue cycle is shorter than three months, host two CCMs before the cycle starts. The first CCM will focus on your heavy revenue periods and the second will focus on the light period following it. This front-loads your strategic work and helps to avoid marketing operations getting de-prioritized during busy periods. (If you are a solo founder, this will change your life.)

Seasonal Businesses

If you are a seasonal business, your business has one revenue cycle per year. In this case, you should use the same strategy above for Cyclical businesses, but just once per year. Host two Campaign Creation Meetings at least three months in advance of the season's start. That is two CCMs per year. The first CCM will be dedicated to in-season direct marketing[28] and the second CCM will be dedicated to off-season branding efforts[29].

---

28 Direct marketing efforts are focused on getting people in the door
29 Branding campaigns are focused on building excitement around the upcoming season and brand loyalty once the season starts

CONVERSIONS: LET'S START AT THE VERY BEGINNING

Now that you've completed your first CCM, you have a plan for launching a strong marketing campaign. Remember what I said earlier—that the point of a campaign is *not* to make sales, but to generate *attention*? Now that you have a plan to get attention, we can finally start talking about getting sales. This is where the third and final piece of your marketing operating system comes in—Conversions. *That's* where the money's at.

Your marketing campaign will get peoples' attention long enough to point them in a direction (via your Call To Action), whether it is to visit a booth at the back of the room, click a link, or watch a video. Everything from that point forward falls under the authority of your **sales funnel.** Your sales funnel picks up where your campaign leaves off by converting your audience's attention into sales.

If you hear the word "funnel" and roll your eyes, or reel back in terror or frustration, that's okay. I get it. If you're afraid that I'm about to point to a funnel as the solution to all your problems, think again. That kind of thinking is what got us into the whole micro-niche mayhem in the first place.

No, I'm just going to use the word *funnel* to explain everything that happens after your campaign's call to action. That's it. Not complicated.

The delineation of your marketing operating system's Campaign and its Conversions lies at the completion of your call to action. As soon as you get someone who engages with your CTA and drops into your funnel, the game changes. When managing a campaign, your goal is to create the best content and find the best channels. But when you're managing a funnel, your goal is to get as many people as possible who completed your call to action to make a purchase. And that means we must look at a very specific type of number.

The Most Important Symbol

What would you say is the most important symbol in marketing?

Take a second to guess.

It's not the exclamation point.
It's not the hashtag symbol.
It's not even the dollar sign.
It's the percentage sign.

The percentage sign is the most important because it represents the most important type of number in marketing: the **conversion rate.**

Conversion rates are numbers that describe the rate at which people are "converting," or taking some sort of action (from clicking a button to buying a product) and moving on to the next step in a funnel.

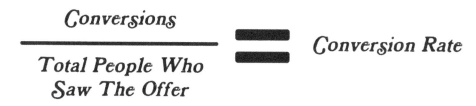

For example, if 1,000 people arrive on your website and 500 of those people convert into leads, you'd have a 50% lead conversion rate.

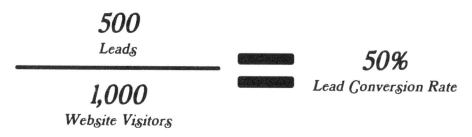

This equation can be applied to any type of action that someone takes in your marketing ecosystem. It can be used for clicks (also known as Click-Through Rate):

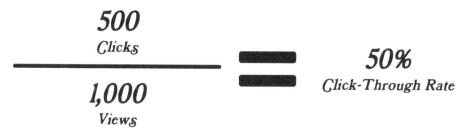

It can be used for video engagement:

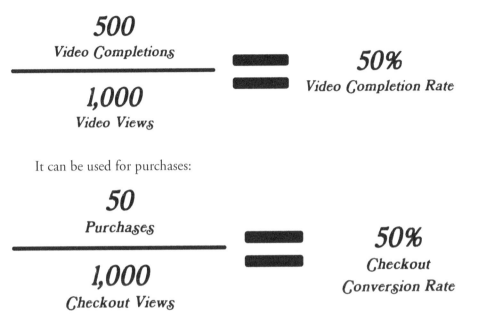

$$\frac{500 \text{ Video Completions}}{1,000 \text{ Video Views}} = 50\% \text{ Video Completion Rate}$$

It can be used for purchases:

$$\frac{50 \text{ Purchases}}{1,000 \text{ Checkout Views}} = 50\% \text{ Checkout Conversion Rate}$$

The top number on the left side of the equation (the numerator) will always be smaller than the bottom number (the denominator). This is because you can never have more conversions than the number of people who saw the offer—that would be like saying 100 people arrived on your checkout page and you received 150 purchases. You can, in some cases, have a 100% conversion rate, but that is rare and usually only happens with low-volume businesses and customers who have exceptionally strong relationships with your company.

Generally speaking, the higher the conversion rate, the better. If you spend $1,000 on ads to send people to your website, you want the click-through rate to be as high as possible. That would mean that you got as many people as possible visiting your website from your ad investment.

Getting a high conversion rate is not always an easy task. Many large companies operate profitably with 3% lead conversion rates on their websites. Expecting a 7% or 10% conversion rate for those pages might be unrealistic, but that doesn't mean it is not worth trying. The process of finding new ways to increase your conversion rates is called **Conversion Rate Optimization**. We'll get to that in a few chapters, but first we need to lay some groundwork.

THE ANATOMY OF A FUNNEL

If a conversion rate represents the act of someone moving from one step in your customer journey to the next, a sales funnel represents your customer journey.

A funnel is an easy metaphor that describes how one step in the customer journey follows another one with a conversion rate at each step. Since conversion rates are less than 100%, fewer and fewer people make their way to later stages in the funnel, with the smallest group of people ending at the bottom of the funnel to ultimately become customers.

Funnels take many forms. Most people think of sales funnels as being exclusively digital—but that's not true. For example, you can have a brick-and-mortar funnel made up of the key actions someone takes as soon as they walk into your store. You can have a B2B service funnel made up of high-touch actions managed by a sales team. You can also have a "typical" digital marketing funnel made up of a series of web pages, order forms, and upsells.

At the end of the day, if you sell anything, you have an established customer journey. That journey has stages, and those stages form the steps of your funnel. You can have a short funnel or a long funnel—it all depends on how long your customer journey is. Shorter funnels are not always easier and longer funnels are not always more profitable.

In the chapters that follow, I'll be using digital marketing funnels as a "proxy" for all types of funnels. If you don't have a digital marketing funnel right now and instead, for example, run a brick-and-mortar location, keep in mind that the concepts remain the same. If you see a digital marketing term you don't understand, you can refer to the Glossary at the back of this book as well as the footnotes I've provided. The point here is to understand the principles of sales funnels and how they work. I guarantee they apply to your business, even if you don't currently have a digital sales funnel in place.

In order to move forward, we must go over some important terminology. I'll be quick but thorough:

The **Top Of The Funnel (TOF)** is where people start your customer journey and become leads. This is where people land after your campaign captures their attention and they engage in your first call to action.

The **Middle Of The Funnel (MOF)** is where your leads are nurtured and getting more excited about buying from you.

The **Bottom Of The Funnel (BOF)** is where those leads pull out their credit card and buy from you. This is also the part of the funnel where **upsells** and **downsells** are added—these are paid offers that new customers can add on to their original order, often without having to re-enter their credit card information. They always appear after someone has purchased their first item, and their purpose is to increase the **Average Transaction Value (ATV)**[30] of the funnel. These are not always required, sometimes profitable, and in some cases counterproductive. Don't be romanticized by upsells and downsells.

As the conversion rates from the TOF to the BOF improve, the funnel performs more efficiently and your Average Transaction Value increases. As that happens it becomes possible for your business to spend more money to acquire new customers. **This ability to reinvest more into acquiring customers is the single most important factor in building a successful marketing strategy.** As Dan Kennedy once wisely said, "The business that can spend the most to acquire a customer wins." When we get to our discussion on conversion rate optimization, you'll discover the path to being able to spend more to acquire your customers.

Top Of Funnel Strategies

The objective of the TOF is to get your first customer conversion. In some cases like an e-commerce website, that conversion will be a purchase. But in most cases, your TOF objective is to convert a visitor into a **lead**[31]. When this is the case, the web page at the top of your funnel is called a **Landing Page**[32]. The landing page contains a form which collects critical contact information on the lead

---

30 ATV, or *Average Transaction Value*, is the average amount of money that your funnel produces per customer. It is calculated by dividing total sales by total customers over the same time period.

31 A lead is considered to be a person who is interested in your product but not yet ready to buy. It is defined by having a new lead record with at least one piece of contact information like an email address or phone number.

32 The landing page is the first page that someone will see after engaging with your marketing campaign's call to action. Visit the Glossary to view the full definition.

(like name and email) and sends that information to your **CRM**[33] (Customer Relationship Management system) for follow-up actions and record-keeping.

In digital marketing, there are all kinds of landing pages you can build. What differentiates them is the offer being made—that is, what the landing page is promising visitors in exchange for filling out the form. If a visitor has decided to pay attention to you long enough to visit the top of your funnel, it is important that you create enough curiosity and provide enough value *on this first step* that they decide it is worth taking the risk of giving you their contact information to see what lies in the second step of the funnel.

I've outlined some of the most popular landing page strategies below to give you an idea of the possibilities. Each of these strategies shares one ultimate goal: getting a visitor to fill out the contact form.

Webinar

A webinar is a live or pre-recorded video presentation. It is designed to broadcast at a predetermined date and time. In the case of pre-recorded webinars, the lead chooses a convenient time to watch the presentation. In the case of live webinars, the scheduling of the webinar is chosen by you, the host.

Webinar platforms like Livestorm, ClickFunnels, WebinarKit, and others are designed to provide this functionality. The benefit of webinars is that the lead can block off an hour or more of their time when it is most convenient for them (rather than going straight into a long presentation, as is the case with a Masterclass or Video Series, which we'll explore shortly).

Typically, live webinars receive the highest level of engagement and attendance out of any free content you can offer. The fact that you (or someone in your company) are going to facilitate a live presentation and interact with the audience is a big benefit to webinar registrants who are interested in asking questions.

Pre-recorded, or "evergreen," webinars are able to be broadcasted multiple times per week, or even per day. They provide a wider range of available scheduling options for your registrants, but often lead to lower engagement. Since the presentation is pre-recorded, attendees don't have to attend live, and any questions that are asked in the chat section will be emailed to you with the attendee's contact information. Almost all webinar platforms support this now.

---

33 A CRM, or *Customer Relationship Management system*, is an online platform that keeps track of your customer records. See the Glossary for an expanded definition.

Given the time commitment of webinars (60-120 minutes), attendees who stick around until the end are "hot" and are considered open to a product pitch. This is one of the main benefits of webinars—you can sell a $2,000 product with relative ease once you have had your attendees' undivided attention for over an hour. There are many trainings out there on how to organize webinars that sell, so I encourage you to check them out at this point if you decide that a webinar is the right strategy for you. One that I really like is Russell Brunson's *Perfect Webinar* training. I would check it out first if you are considering producing a webinar.

Worksheet

Worksheets (also called Work*books*, depending on the length) are documents containing exercises or templates that the lead can immediately access and use. These are typically best for businesses which provide training programs or certifications. Worksheets are most commonly provided in PDF format, but you can use whatever format you like.

Worksheets are a great way to deliver a valuable exercise or lesson that your lead can guide themselves through. If properly designed, the worksheet will help the lead gain a valuable insight as well as build a deeper understanding of what your company does.

Since the worksheet is downloadable to your lead's computer, that means it also brings them *offline*. You won't be able to track when the lead prints or fills out your worksheet, which means you need to have an automated system that follows up with your lead to make sure they have actually used the worksheet. I also recommend placing a call to action at the bottom of the worksheet to entice your lead further down your funnel. It is for this reason that I recommend having a Tripwire Page[34] (more on that soon) after any worksheet Landing Page. Without an immediate digital "next step," you'll end up causing a lot of leads to fall out of your funnel.

---

34 Tripwires are low-cost, low risk paid offers that you can make to a new lead. They are designed to lower the barrier to entry into your customer base and they help convince a new lead to pull out their credit card and give your company a try. The first transaction is a critical moment in your customer journey, and it immediately increases the likelihood that they will purchase from you again.

Video Series

The video series was first thought up over fifteen years ago by a guy named Jeff Walker, creator of the *Product Launch Blueprint*. Since then, video series have evolved into highly functional mini sites that deliver lessons in an episodic format to anyone looking to solve a highly painful challenge. You can create a video series about anything from gardening techniques to business strategies.

Most video series are comprised of four to five videos which each last between twenty and thirty minutes. A lead will register on the Landing Page to gain access to the video series, and, upon registration, they will be redirected to a page that shows them the first video. They can see a navigation outlining the videos they have yet to see, but they cannot yet access them.

This is where the real value of the video series comes in. The *limited access* to the rest of the video series causes curiosity which, in turn, translates into a high expectation of value. After 24 hours, the next video is unlocked and emailed to the lead, and so on for the next few days until they reach the final video in the series. Each video builds on the content in the previous video in order to create continuity and psychological momentum for the lead, who is (hopefully) feeling like they are making great progress toward figuring out their problem. The final video delivers the last piece of the puzzle, fulfilling the big promise originally made on the Landing Page. It also, importantly, contains a *pitch*. This could be a pitch for an event, a training program, a service, a consultation, or some other product that you want to sell to your leads.

Given the multi-day time commitment of a video series, this tool has relatively high conversion rates for those leads who stick with the video series until completion. Anyone who makes time day after day to come back to your video series is clearly demonstrating that they are committed to solving their problem. Given the fact that you provide so much value in advance of any purchase (it will end up being around 90-120 minutes of content), by the time they reach the final video in the series, it is appropriate (and in some cases expected) for you to make a pitch. The price range for products you can easily pitch using a video series is about the same as a webinar, which currently is between $500 and $5,000. Anything above that requires a phone call in the process (unless you have an exceptionally strong brand).

Quiz

Quizzes are a new and successful form of lead generation strategy. Using quiz technology like Interact, Outgrow, Leadquizzes, and Bucket.io (among many others), you can create a super-engaging and personalized experience for your visitors.

You can build a quiz around any topic—but it should, in all cases, deliver a valuable and personalized insight for your leads. I have built quizzes in all kinds of industries, from leadership training to lab testing, and the one common factor of success was thinking through the *results* we provided.

The results are what drive the demand for a quiz in the first place. If you have ever seen those quizzes that promise to help you "Find out what Disney princess you are," you know the feeling of expecting some kind of outcome. You might wonder if you are Princess Jasmine from *Aladdin*, or Ariel from *The Little Mermaid*, or Cinderella. That *expectation* of a particular result is what makes quizzes so compelling. We always *want* to know the answer.

This is why planning a quiz is so important. In all my testing around quizzes, the design and copywriting of the quiz Landing Page turned out to be relatively unimportant. In one interesting experiment, I had Facebook ad traffic skip the Landing Page altogether and go right into the first quiz question—and we ended up getting *higher* completion rates than we had *with* the Landing Page and all its fancy design and copywriting.

This is because the *expectation of the result* is what drives quiz completions. The promise of the quiz is simple. People get it. And as soon as they understand what you are promising, they are already ready to answer the first question. So, the challenge is not building the best landing page possible—it is building the best *quiz* you possibly can. That means thinking through the results *first* and forming the questions in a way that lets your quiz software categorize people around your results.

Let's say I was building a quiz that promised to help people figure out the best things to plant in their garden. I would start with the results—vegetables, fruits, flowers, and mushrooms—and form my questions in a way that helps my quiz software categorize answers. Some examples could be:

What climate do you live in?
Answer 1: Arid
Answer 2: Humid

What is your goal for gardening?
Answer 1: Grow food
Answer 2: Have a beautiful garden or yard

Each of the answers would add points to a particular result. For example, if someone said they live in a humid climate, the *Mushrooms* result would get one point. By the end of the quiz, the result with the most points would win. The quiz taker would enter their contact information to see their results and then would be redirected to a results page that you have created which tells them more about their result and provides next steps, products, or video lessons built specifically around their result. This personalized experience is exciting for the quiz taker and leads to high conversion rates further down the funnel.

Whitepaper

Whitepapers are the simplest and most traditional form of Landing Page offer. While they have lost popularity over the years with the rise of more engaging and interactive offers, they still have a place. They are ideal for market research companies, enterprise software companies, and other organizations who are interested in sharing case studies and quantitative research with their leads.

That being said, whitepapers have low engagement rates. Like worksheets, since they are downloadable files, they allow for people to drop out of your funnel more easily and lose momentum. That is why it is important to have a strong "next step" on your Thank You Page or Delivery Page, such as a consultation request form, application, tripwire purchase, or something else that keeps leads moving through the funnel until they reach a transaction or some other conversion that qualifies them for a stronger follow-up like a phone call.

Free Trial

Free trials are ideal for software companies that can quickly onboard new users as well as membership programs. Depending on your business model and financials, your free trial can be anywhere from a few days to a few weeks. Regardless of the time period of the trial, it is important that you decide whether you will collect payment information upfront.

Collecting credit card information on the lead's signup will drastically reduce your conversion rates, but it will also increase your collections once trials expire.

It is **imperative**, if you do collect payment information upfront, that you make it abundantly clear when (and for how much) you will automatically charge your customer's credit card, as well as how they can cancel before the trial expires.

If you don't collect payment information upfront, you can expect much higher conversion rates to your trial. But then there's a new challenge which is getting trial users to enter their payment information before the trial expires. This requires a well-thought-out email, app notification, phone, or other sequence that encourages trial users to upgrade their account before their access is revoked.

Demo

Demonstrations are another ideal Landing Page strategy for software companies. Instead of offering leads a self-guided free trial, you could schedule a time to meet on a video call to walk them through your platform, answer their questions, and make your pitch. In some cases, if you have a clear understanding of the demo process, you can pre-record the demo and allow new leads to watch instantly.

Demos are a low-risk option for funnel visitors, but they also have a lower level of instant gratification than free trials since the lead can't interact with the software themselves. This makes demos ideal for software companies that have high setup costs for new users or companies whose platforms are a little more complicated to learn. This is why enterprise software companies like Salesforce use demos instead of free trials—jumping right into the platform would be overwhelming for new leads, making it likely that they would become immediately overwhelmed with a free trial.

Masterclass

Masterclasses are pre-recorded videos that last between 45-90 minutes. Leads get instant access to them upon registration on the Landing Page and in some cases their access to the Masterclass is limited to a certain period of time in order to create urgency around an offer that is made in the Masterclass video itself.

Masterclasses are designed to accomplish in roughly an hour what a Video Series accomplishes over the course of multiple days. This means that Masterclasses are absolutely *packed* with value, designed for immediate implementation, and focused on helping your leads achieve an early "win." It also means that Masterclasses are similar in nature to Webinars. They share the same characteristics, except that Masterclasses are accessed instantly and have no interactivity with the host.

In some cases, Masterclasses can be split into multiple parts, in which case you will have a hybrid between a Video Series and a Masterclass. You can design a Masterclass in any way that you want, including making the first part of the Masterclass available for free and the remainder behind a paywall (in other words, you can give leads a free trial to a paid Masterclass). The choice is yours.

No matter how you structure your Masterclass, it is important to keep in mind what your "next step" will be. The Masterclass is designed to keep your leads' full attention for a long period of time. This gives you an opportunity to make an offer to buy your product or enter the next step of your funnel.

Brick-and-Mortar Options

The TOF strategies above are all exclusive to the digital marketing realm. If you are running a physical location, your strategy will be different, but the principle remains the same. In many cases, a storefront's TOF goal would be to get someone to walk through the front door. Consider what kinds of promises or enticements you can offer pedestrians in order to pique their curiosity. Free samples, window displays, store promotions, and sidewalk sales are all examples of TOF strategies that will capture the attention of passersby.

The biggest advantage of having a physical location is that you can engage multiple senses at the same time. People can walk into the store, pick things up, have friendly conversations with your staff, and do all kinds of other things that are otherwise bland and boring in an online setting. Take advantage of this opportunity—those are all Experiential mediums that you may not be leveraging.

Value In Advance

The purpose of all these strategies is to deliver *value in advance*. That means you are creating something that visitors can get for free, which demonstrates that you have a valuable product and a reliable brand. These offers are not designed to give away everything you have, but they should "feel" like you are giving away something that you could otherwise charge for. That is the whole point—if the visitor doesn't feel like they are getting something truly valuable (rather than just some throwaway piece of content), they won't convert into a lead.

Once a visitor converts into a lead, they move on to the second step of your funnel. This is a critical moment in the customer journey—one in which they are deciding whether the risk paid off in giving you their contact information (or, in the case of a physical location, their attention and willingness to walk into your store).

There are three types of pages you can create at this stage: **Thank You** pages, **Delivery** pages, and **Tripwire** pages.

Thank You Pages are, as the name suggests, a step of the funnel in which you simply express gratitude for the person converting on the Landing Page. This is a place to provide them with next steps, including instructions on how to access the offer they requested by filling out the Landing Page form. In the case of a webinar offer, for example, the Thank You Page will contain instructions on how to watch the webinar at the date and time they chose on the webinar registration form.

Delivery Pages are designed to immediately provide access to the offer they were promised on the Landing Page. In the case of a masterclass, for example, the second step of the funnel would be a Delivery Page that contains an embedded video of the masterclass itself. If you are providing them with a downloadable whitepaper or worksheet, you can add a button to download the file to their computer. In some cases, it is better to automatically email your lead the downloadable file and use the Delivery Page to provide a thank-you message and make a one-time offer (in this case, you don't have a Delivery Page—you have a Tripwire Page). Be careful here, though, because if you don't manage that transition carefully, it will be a bait-and-switch.

The term "tripwire" is used in digital marketing to describe the first transaction someone makes with you in your sales funnel. The metaphor is appropriate. The tripwire offer, like a real tripwire, triggers something.

Of course, in war, the tripwire sets off a bomb, so we lose the metaphor at that point. In marketing, however, the tripwire offer sets off a series of psychological effects that the customer experiences in their journey through your funnel. Specifically, by making their first purchase with you, they have crossed the threshold of *considering* whether you are trustworthy enough to buy from. By making their tripwire purchase, they have *decided* that you have something worth their time and money.

Tripwire Pages, as a result, are designed from the ground up to do one thing: convert leads into paid sales. That means the tripwire *offer*, the thing you are actually selling for money, should be exceptionally valuable. More valuable even than the offer you made on the Landing Page. Some examples of tripwire offers are discounted event tickets, content packages, VIP consultations, and online memberships.

Two important distinguishing features of tripwire offers are *scarcity* and *exclusivity*. Tripwire offers are often made with a strict time limit—this is often where you'll see countdown timers at work. Scarcity creates value which, in turn, raises the likelihood that your new lead will convert into a customer by completing a purchase. Exclusivity also enters the mix when you make an offer that new leads cannot get anywhere else. This is usually communicated by labeling your tripwire offer as a *new member special* or something similar. When a valuable tripwire offer is made to new leads and they know they can't get it anywhere else or at any other time, the likelihood rises that they will take the leap and buy.

Bad Offers

The most important thing to remember when creating tripwire offers is that the value of the offer is what ultimately leads to the sale. No amount of scarcity or exclusivity can help a bad offer. That is why it is critical to put a lot of thought and care into building something of immense value to offer new leads. After they purchase your tripwire, they will be met with their first moment of split-second buyers' remorse (which is completely natural), and the value of your tripwire must be so high that their excitement outweighs any questions around whether they made the right decision or not—in fact, it must be high enough that their excitement immediately overpowers the buyer's remorse and leads them to want more from you. Make your tripwire offer unique to your business, packed with value, and immediately actionable, and you will be well on your way to monetizing your funnel.

IMPORTANT:

It is possible that a Tripwire Page is **not** appropriate for your sales funnel. For example, if you operate in a high-touch or high-ticket market in which one-on-one relationships are essential, tripwire offers can create the wrong impression. A good rule of thumb is that if your customer acquisition process is quite long, or you expect that you are going to get on the phone with a lead before any initial purchase is made, you shouldn't use a Tripwire Page, since it could put the relationship at risk. This is most common in non-productized (or boutique) service businesses that work on custom projects.

THE FLAW IN SALES FUNNELS

As I mentioned before, a funnel represents all the steps of your customer journey. If each of those steps has a conversion rate, then you can think of a funnel simply as a stack of conversion rates.

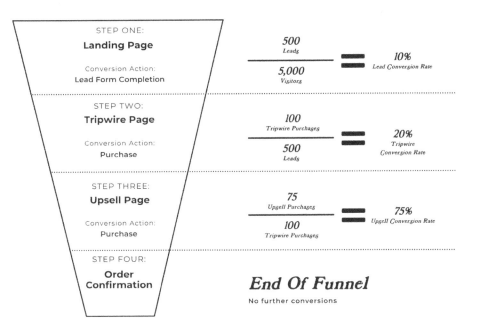

The funnel in the graphic above is made up of four steps: a Landing Page, Tripwire Page, Upsell Page[35], and Order Confirmation Page. There are conver-

---

35 Also known as a One-Time Offer (OTO) page, an Upsell Page provides a one-time opportunity to add another product to the original tripwire product order. Since these pages are displayed immediately after a tripwire purchase, new customers' credit card information is stored in the purchasing system, so they can click one button to add the Upsell offer to their order without re-entering their payment information. Funnel software like ClickFunnels and Samcart make this possible.

sion rates for every step other than the Order Confirmation Page, which is the end of the funnel and, thus, contains no further transactions.

Notice that the numerator (the top number in the division formula) in each step becomes the denominator (the bottom number) in the next step. For example, leads appear as the numerator in Step One and then move to the denominator in Step Two.

This is because every conversion on every funnel step feeds people to the next step in the funnel. For example, everyone who purchases on the Tripwire Page is automatically redirected to the Upsell Page. This is why the funnel layout is so helpful—everything moves downward. Unfortunately, the funnel visualization loses its value when we start to ask "what-if" questions and make predictions:

What if I added an Upsell?

What conversion rate do I need if I want to make 1,000 more sales?

What ad spend would I need if I want to get 100 leads per day?

I will illustrate why this is a challenge using the graphic below. Let's say we have 5,000 visitors to our funnel and have a target of 75 upsell sales. Here's what that looks like in the funnel visualization:

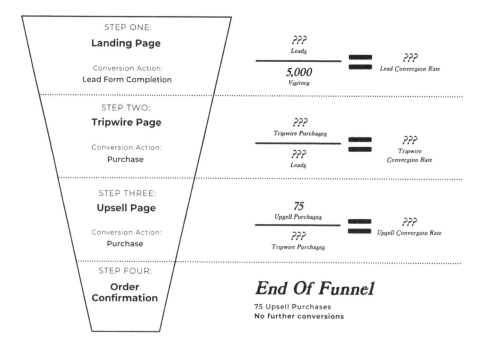

See all those question marks? Not very helpful.

This is the point where the funnel visualization falls apart. We need something a bit more structured in order to answer our "what-if" question without turning our brains into goop.

Over the years, I have created an easy way around this problem called the **Funnel Grid.** This is a simple, back-of-the-napkin method for making funnel calculations. **This is one of the most important skills you will learn in this book.** The ability to make funnel calculations will help you speak intelligently with smart marketers and spot unskilled marketers a mile away. The reason this skill is so important is because it is *not* intuitive. Don't get me wrong—it *is* simple from a math standpoint. But it's definitely not intuitive. Marketers who have not done their homework have not learned this, much less used it in practice.

A Funnel Grid for a four-step sales funnel looks like this:

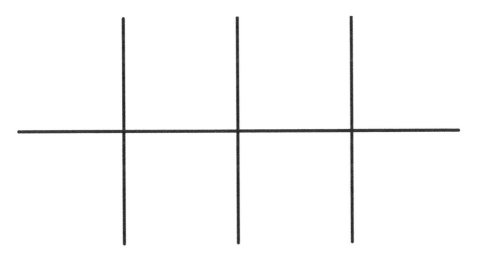

Four columns for four funnel steps. Simple enough.

Now we will add labels for the funnel steps as well as for the two rows which will contain two types of numbers: Unique Visitors[36] and Conversion Rate:

---

36   *Unique visitors* is a term that describes the total number of people who visited a step in your funnel. The word "unique" is important because total website visit metrics are often inflated when a visitor refreshes a page or visits the same page multiple times.

STEP ONE: Landing Page	STEP TWO: Tripwire Page	STEP THREE: Upsell Page	STEP FOUR: Order Confirmation

(Unique Visitors / Conversion Rate grid — empty)

Then, last but not least, we put in the numbers for our sales funnel. To do that, we first place our Unique Visitors for each funnel step in the top row using our historical data:

STEP ONE: Landing Page	STEP TWO: Tripwire Page	STEP THREE: Upsell Page	STEP FOUR: Order Confirmation
5,000	500	100	75

(Unique Visitors top row / Conversion Rate bottom row)

Great!

We can now see that 5,000 people visited the TOF step (our Landing Page) and 75 people made it all the way through to the BOF (the Order Confirmation).

Now we can place the conversion rates in the bottom row. We can easily calculate the conversion rates without even going back to our website analytics—for example, we see that 500 people landed on the Tripwire Page, and that was out of 5,000 people visiting the Landing Page. 500 divided by 5,000 is 10%. We do that for each spot in the Conversion Rate row:

	STEP ONE: Landing Page	STEP TWO: Tripwire Page	STEP THREE: Upsell Page	STEP FOUR: Order Confirmation
Unique Visitors	5,000	500	100	75
Conversion Rate	10%	20%	75%	

Note that the bottom right box is empty. This is because the Order Confirmation Page has no further call to action, so there is no conversion rate. It's the end of the funnel.

Each traffic number is the product[37] of the traffic number and conversion rate to its left. So we have this zig-zag flow through the Funnel Grid. Here's what it looks like when we move from left to right:

---

37   The resulting number when you multiply two numbers together

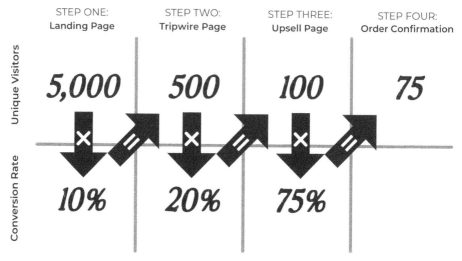

Now things get interesting.

Division is the opposite process of multiplication[38], so we can reverse these calculations by moving right to left:

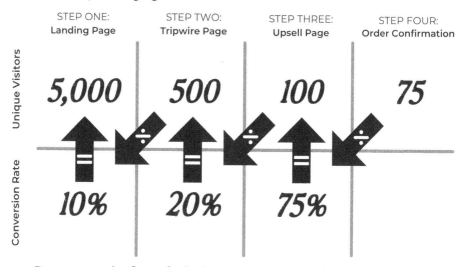

By reversing the flow of calculations, we changed the calculation symbols. Instead of multiplying from left to right, we are now dividing from right to left.

Using this process, we can make quick and easy calculations on our funnel. We can predict what will happen if traffic or conversion rates change and we can answer "what-if" questions when we are considering adding a product to our funnel.

---

38   Known as an *inverse operation* for all the math nerds out there

Expanded Explanation

If the explanation of the Funnel Grid above doesn't make much sense, read through the expanded guide below. If you are following along just fine, you can skip this section and move onto the next chapter.

If you need a little more explanation, let's pause and go through the Funnel Grid process one more time in more detail.

The process of multiplying and dividing are mathematical opposites. If I multiply 2 by 4, I get 8. The 8 is the result of combining the first two numbers. To put it differently, the 8 can be thought of as still containing the 2 and the 4. Here's a way to think about it in terms of mathematical variables:

$$A \times B = AB$$
$$2 4 8$$

If I were to somehow split the A and the B away from each other, I would get the 2 and the 4. This is what division does—it's the mechanism we use to un-multiply. It splits a multiplied number apart.

This comes in handy when we're dealing with funnel conversion rates because the ingredients of each conversion rate are made up of traffic numbers. Here's a simple way of looking at it through the lens of a Funnel Grid:

	STEP ONE: Landing Page	STEP TWO: Tripwire Page	STEP THREE: Upsell Page	STEP FOUR: Order Confirmation
Unique Visitors	A	AB		
Conversion Rate	B			

In the case of the graphic above, multiplying A (the Landing Page traffic) by B (the Landing Page Conversion Rate gives us AB (the resulting **Leads**[39]). If we keep going, we can see how the numbers keep multiplying by each other:

STEP ONE: Landing Page	STEP TWO: Tripwire Page	STEP THREE: Upsell Page	STEP FOUR: Order Confirmation
A	**AB**	**ABC**	**ABCD**
B	**C**	**D**	

(Vertical axis: Unique Visitors / Conversion Rate)

Here is what it looks like with the left-to-right calculation flow added:

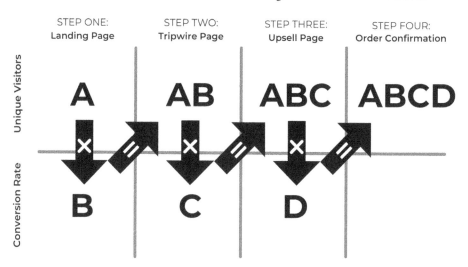

---

39 Leads are typically created during the conversion of a Landing Page visitor. This is often, but not always, the case.

As we get deeper into the funnel, the resulting traffic numbers are multiplied by more and more percentages (B, C, and D), which brings the total number down. By the time we calculate ABCD, we are left with the smallest number of them all: the original Landing Page traffic multiplied by every funnel step's conversion rate (which ends up being the traffic to the Order Confirmation).

Another way to look at this is that B x C x D (or BCD) will give you the overall **Funnel Conversion Rate**. This is also known as the **Click-To-Sale Conversion Rate**.

I sometimes like to use the grey box as a place to put the Funnel Conversion Rate. That is just another shorthand trick I use to save time and give me a good high-level view of how the funnel is performing as a whole.

	STEP ONE: Landing Page	STEP TWO: Tripwire Page	STEP THREE: Upsell Page	STEP FOUR: Order Confirmation
Unique Visitors	*5,000*	*500*	*100*	*75*
Conversion Rate	*10%*	*20%*	*75%*	*10% × 20% × 75% =* *1.5%*

(Side note: If you are having trouble with using percentages on a calculator, move the decimal point on every percentage value to the left two spaces. So 10% becomes 0.10 and 25% becomes 0.25. This is the proper mathematical value for percentages.)

Now that we have moved forward on the Funnel Grid, what does it look like to move backwards?

As I mentioned above, when we switch directions on the Funnel Grid, the calculations reverse. Multiplication turns into division. Let's look at a simple example:

STEP ONE: Landing Page	STEP TWO: Tripwire Page	STEP THREE: Upsell Page	STEP FOUR: Order Confirmation
Unique Visitors 5,000	500	A	AB
Conversion Rate 10%	20%	B	

When we want to deconstruct a number like AB, we can do so by dividing it by either of its counterparts, A or B.

$$AB \div A = B$$
$$8 \quad\quad 2 \quad\quad 4$$

$$AB \div B = A$$
$$8 \quad\quad 4 \quad\quad 2$$

Whichever way you divide, you'll end up with A and B by themselves. Let's try applying this to a real-world example.

You have a three-step funnel with the following traffic numbers:

	STEP ONE: Landing Page	STEP TWO: Tripwire Page	STEP THREE: Order Confirmation
Unique Visitors	846	211	18
Conversion Rate			

We then add in conversion rates:

	STEP ONE: Landing Page	STEP TWO: Tripwire Page	STEP THREE: Order Confirmation
Unique Visitors	846	211	18
Conversion Rate	24.9%	8.5%	

Now let's say you just created another product and want to add an Upsell Page.

You'd place the Upsell Page after the Tripwire Page (which is typically designed to be the first point of purchase).

If you had a target of 5 Upsell sales, and you didn't have the budget or time to increase your Landing Page traffic, what would your upsell conversion rate need to be?

Well, now that you have another step in the Funnel Grid, your old Order Confirmation traffic would turn into the traffic for the new Upsell Page. Let's put into the Funnel Grid along with our goal of 5 Upsell sales:

	STEP ONE: Landing Page	STEP TWO: Tripwire Page	STEP THREE: Upsell Page	STEP FOUR: Order Confirmation
Unique Visitors	*846*	*211*	*18*	*5*
Conversion Rate	*24.9%*	*8.5%*	*???*	

In order to hit the target of 5 Upsell Sales, we need to hit a certain conversion rate on the Upsell Page in order to turn 18 visitors into 5 sales. So we would need to divide the Order Confirmation traffic (our goal) of 5 by the Upsell Page traffic of 18:

$$AB \div A = B$$
$$5 \qquad 18 \qquad ?$$

So we pull out our calculator and find the value for B, which ends up being 0.277, or 27.7%.

$$AB \div A = B$$

$$5 \qquad\qquad 18 \qquad\qquad 27.7\%$$

Great!

We now know that our Upsell Page *must* have a conversion rate of 27.7% or higher in order for us to hit our goal of 5 upsell sales. We found that by using what we already knew: the traffic numbers before and after the sale. Knowing this, we would be able to launch the new Upsell Page and know what numbers we need to hit.

THE MARKETER'S SCIENTIFIC METHOD

"No amount of experimentation can ever prove me right;
a single experiment can prove me wrong."
Albert Einstein

Now that you have the Funnel Grid in your tool belt to review your funnel's performance on the fly, you can also start to spot areas where your funnel is underperforming. These are called **bottlenecks.** They are places where people seem to get *stuck* in your funnel. In other words, bottlenecks are places where more people than normal are falling out of your buying process. When this kind of thing happens, it is really hard to get them back.

Conversion Rate Optimization (CRO) is the process of finding and fixing bottlenecks in your funnel. As you spot funnel steps that have lower conversion rates than you would like, you can use CRO techniques to raise them. CRO techniques are entirely based on running **split tests,** which are experiments designed to "try out" new forms of your copywriting, design, and customer experience on specific steps of your funnel. These split tests (also known as A/B tests) are carried out using the tried-and-true research process known as the scientific method.

The Scientific Method

You may remember the Scientific Method from elementary school. Yes, it's the same one. Scientists follow the same steps to run an experiment, regardless of if they are running a booth at a science fair or in charge of a $5 billion particle accelerator. Those steps are:

1. Ask A Question
2. Conduct Research
3. Form A Hypothesis
4. Run An Experiment

5. Collect & Analyze Data
6. Report Conclusions

Six beautiful steps.

For me, there is something calming about the scientific method. There is an objectivity that you know you can rely on—it wipes the slate clean of emotional decisions and clears out ulterior motives. To someone like me who ran an agency for almost a decade, science became the strongest defense I had against emotional arguments from colleagues and clients (and often myself) who thought they knew everything.

You may be in the same boat; you might have someone breathing down your neck expecting you to have all the answers, or thinking they do. Or you yourself might feel like *you* need to have all the answers to your marketing problems. Marketing science is here to lift that burden off your shoulders. Being a Marketing Scientist means you don't *need* to have all the answers—because you have the skills to find the right answer at the right time.

Let's explore each step of the scientific method through the lens of a Marketing Scientist. Some of this material may seem familiar to you, but I've written this all in a way that can be directly applied to your marketing and CRO efforts.

STEP ONE: ASK THE RIGHT QUESTION

This is the first and most important step of the scientific method. The question sets the stage for your experiment, and it shines a light on exactly what you are trying to figure out. That's why it is so important to get right.

The right question will lead you to some amazing insights—but the wrong question can result in inconclusive or misleading data. The key to asking the right question is to think ahead to the target data point, or **Key Performance Indicator**[40] (KPI) that you want the question to affect, and then to decide what you are going to change in order to test your theory—that is known as your **variable**[41].

During an experiment, two or more versions of the same funnel step are put in a contest against each other. The original funnel step, known as the **control**, still receives traffic, but some of that traffic is diverted to one or more **variants**[42], which are versions of the control with changes made to the variable. In the illustration below, we are testing a landing page to see if a new layout will generate a higher conversion rate.

---

40 The marketing performance metric your experiment is designed to improve
41 The variable represents the element of your funnel that you want to change in order to get a certain result. In marketing funnel terms, your variable typically falls into one of three categories: copywriting, design, and technical functionality.
42 A variant (also known as a *treatment*) is a version of the experiment's control. For example, if you are testing the layout of a landing page, the current landing page (with no changes) is used as the experiment control while a duplicated version of the control, with some edit made based on your variable, is used as the variant.

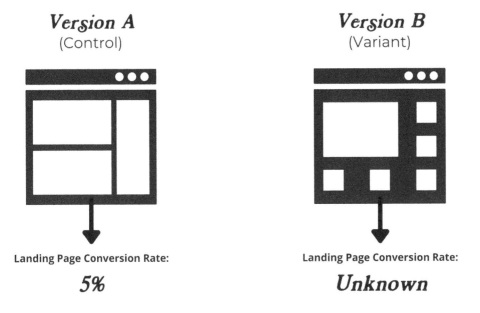

Version A
(Control)

Version B
(Variant)

Landing Page Conversion Rate:

5%

Landing Page Conversion Rate:

Unknown

Let's take a look the question we would ask around the illustrated split test above:

"Does a different page layout increase the landing page conversion rate?"

Do you see the variable?

It is the page layout.

Do you see the KPI?

It is the landing page conversion rate.

Both elements of the experiment—the variable and the KPI—are clearly identified.

Now notice the **phrasing** of the question. It implies a *yes* or *no* answer.

This is important. Your question must imply a certain type of answer. There are two types of questions you can ask: Binary Questions (which result in a *yes* or *no* answer) and Selection Questions (which result in a *"this one"* type of answer). Let's explore each in more detail.

Binary Questions

A Binary Question always results in a *yes* or *no* answer. Binary Questions are used in experiments with one variant. They begin with words such as "Does," "Do," or "Will." For example:

- Will adding a discount code pop-up in the bottom corner increase checkouts?

- Does a single column layout increase time on page?
- Do photos with people decrease the bounce rate of the home page?

Binary Questions are ideal if you are testing a **significant variable**. An example of a significant variable is page layout—a lot of resources are needed to create a new page design, so it would not be an efficient use of time to test all *possible* page layouts—thus, you can test the original page against a variant page with a different layout by using a Binary Question.

Selection Questions

A selection question results in an answer that essentially says, *"this one."* Selection questions are used in split tests with more than one variant. They usually begin with the word "Which." For example:

- Which landing page design has the best lead conversion rate?
- Which form length creates the lowest bounce rate?
- Which thumbnail image results in the highest clicks?

Each of these questions will result in an answer that points to a specific variant that outperformed all the others. Selection Questions are ideal when you want to test multiple versions of the variable, such as testing multiple headlines at the same time.

If you had four landing page headline variants in addition to your control, you would tell your split testing software to split traffic into 20% increments. That would send an equal number of visitors to the control and each of the four variants. Once you have enough data, a winner will emerge—and that will become the new headline for 100% of landing page traffic.

Poorly Formed Questions

Avoid open-ended questions, such as those that begin with *"How"* or *"What."* When you ask those types of questions, your experiment will be inconclusive. For example, if I were to ask the question, *"What button color increases the click-through rate of the checkout page?"* I won't be able to proceed with the scientific method because I've implied an infinite number of colors to test. When there is no variable, anything can be a variable. That's not how experiments work.

If, on the other hand, I changed my wording to *"**Which** button color increases the click-through rate of the checkout page?"* then we are onto something. This new wording implies that there is a finite list of colors that I want to test.

It opens up the possibility for the experiment to give an answer along the lines of *"this color works best."*

As we will see shortly, the structure of the scientific method allows you to turn data into an answer to your question, but that question is going to either say *yes, no,* or *this one.* Structuring your question in such a way that you get one of those three answers will ensure that you run a proper experiment.

Two Ways To Form A Good Question

Good questions are led by curiosity. They can arise in all kinds of ways, but there are two particular methods that are of use to Marketing Scientists. The first is **Pattern Recognition**, which is asking a question based on a pattern you notice. The second is **Creative Brainstorming**, which is when you think of a new way of applying existing knowledge to a new scenario.

Pattern Recognition

In the early 1900s, a psychologist named Bluma Zeigarnik was having lunch at a local restaurant. She was friends with the waitress, so they chatted for a few minutes. They ended up discussing the other diners at the restaurant. Bluma realized that the waitress had an uncanny ability to remember every single thing ordered by the other diner patrons. After asking a few pointed questions, she realized that the waitress's memory wasn't as strong as she thought—the waitress was apparently only able to remember the orders of tables that hadn't yet paid their checks.

Bluma was intrigued—she had spotted a pattern. So, she went back to her office and began an experiment to find out if this was a larger, more universal pattern among humans. That experiment led to the discovery of a new cognitive effect, known today as the Zeigarnik Effect, named after Bluma. She discovered that human beings are wired to feel a psychological weight when they are responsible for unfinished tasks, and that weight is released when the task is finished. The side effect of this "weight" is higher recall of the tasks that have remained unfinished. In short, we have better memory of incomplete tasks than we do of those we have completed.

Bluma Zeigarnik recognized a pattern in her interaction with the waitress and that pattern triggered a series of questions that ultimately led to her experiment to find out whether more people demonstrate the same behavior. This is an example of the **Pattern Recognition** path of asking a scientific question.

When you see a pattern in your marketing reports, or even in the behavior of your customers, that should make you pause and think. Odds are it could be something important. That is the first step to forming a great experiment. Take a close look at how your leads behave, how they talk, and what they say are their biggest challenges. There may be some hidden gems that can be used as the basis of asking an interesting question.

Creative Brainstorming

A few years ago, my agency's team came across Bluma Zeigarnik's research. We started thinking of ways that we could use the Zeigarnik Effect to improve a customer's experience and increase our client's checkout page performance. So we asked the question:

"Can the Zeigarnik effect be practically and ethically used to reduce cart abandonment?"

This is an example of forming a scientific question through **Creative Brainstorming**. The question above had a KPI (cart abandonment), but it didn't have a variable. We weren't ready to move forward in the scientific method yet. That's where the brainstorming came in.

We knew we had this thing called the Zeigarnik Effect, and we knew that it could be ethically utilized in the design of the checkout process. The question was what *form* the variable took. So we began to do some research.

Eventually, we came across Dove's *Campaign For Real Beauty*. In it, Dove shared images of women of all ethnicities, shapes, ages, and sizes. Next to their pictures, there were two unchecked boxes that forced the viewer to mentally "tick" one answer off.

There was a picture of a grey-haired woman in her 50's. The two boxes next to her said:

☐ Grey?
☐ Gorgeous?

There was a picture of a wrinkle-faced woman in her 70's. The two boxes next to her said:

☐ Wrinkled?
☐ Wonderful?

There was a picture of an Asian woman in her 30's. The two boxes next to her said:

☐ Single Eyelids?

☐ Twice As Nice?

There was a picture of a woman with small breasts. The two boxes next to her said:

☐ Flat?

☐ Flattering?

There was a picture of a woman with a short haircut. The two boxes next to her said:

☐ Boy?

☐ Babe?

We went through all of these ads and thought—how cool! Dove was using the mental wiring in our brains to trigger the Zeigarnik Effect and have us decide which option we would check (communicating their Big Idea along the way).

We thought we could do this, too.

We asked, "what if we designed a set of three checked-off boxes that reinforced the steps the customer already took and then added in a final un-checked box for the purchase they're about to make?"

Then we thought, *"hey, let's **animate** the process of checking off the boxes so the customer notices it."* We wouldn't just let someone mentally check the boxes for themselves—we would do it for them as it happened automatically in their heads.

What emerged was what is now known at Vivid Labs as the Zeigarnik Process Animation. Here is what a basic version looks like:

☑ **You registered for the download**

☑ **You purchased the starter pack**

☑ **Your access email is on its way**

☐ Your upgrade is pending...

On a webpage, those checkboxes are animated and appear one at a time, moving down until the visitor sees the final unchecked box. Zeigarnik's research told us that we feel relieved when a task is completed, so the three already-checked boxes are a sort of congratulations and thank-you for the page visitor while the final unchecked box is a reminder that they still have one step to go, thus creating tension.

Although simple, this animation caused checkout page visitors to mentally zoom out, consider the journey they have completed already, and then feel the pressure to complete the full process. And it worked, too. Checkout conversions rose by over 20% overnight.

This is a simple animation you can create and export as a GIF animation. Feel free to use ours—you can even use our own Canva template at teamvivid. com/animation. (That will send you to Canva.com and automatically add the template to your account. Feel free to customize and use it.)

This case study is a perfect example of **Creative Brainstorming**. We came across new information, formed a creative idea of how to leverage it in a different way, and asked the question of whether or not it would raise the performance of our checkout page. The animation became our variable—we literally *invented a new variable* based on inspiration from our research—and allowed ourselves to proceed with the scientific method, fully-formed question in hand.

STEP TWO: DO YOUR RESEARCH

"Every brilliant experiment, like every great work of art,
starts with an act of imagination."
Jonah Lehrer

O nce you have identified your question, you will have to conduct research
to inform the structure of your experiment. The depth of this research
depends on the source of your question.

If your question was based on **Creative Brainstorming**, then you have
already done a lot of the work. In the example above with our application of the
Zeigarnik Effect to a checkout page, we already had the research in hand and
were simply testing a new application. Our question was:

Does the Zeigarnik Process Animation increase the checkout page conversion rate?

The only research we had to do was to find out if the Zeigarnik Effect could
be applied to a checkout page, if it was ethical to do so, and whether it had been
tried before (this is where the Dove campaign appeared on our radar).

More times than not, in marketing, you will be using the Creative Brainstorm approach. Applying existing research to your marketing is simpler, faster,
and often more effective than the Pattern Recognition method of question-form-
ing. There is a ton of research out there about how the brain works, why people
buy, and other forms of cognitive research that can give you all kinds of ideas of
ways to improve the performance of your marketing.

But, if your question is based on **Pattern Recognition**, then you have a little
more work to do. You have spotted a pattern, but you are still starting out with
very little knowledge of what is going on, which means you have to develop a
theory. In the same way that Einstein used his imagination to develop his own

theories, you have to use your imagination and try to come up with possible explanations for what is going on.

The primary function of a theory is to identify variables and propose logical relationships between those variables and your target data point. To explain this, I will provide an example.

An Example Of Pattern Recognition Research

Let's say that you run an online toy store that sells model trains and cars. You've been poring over your website data and have noticed that, over the past six months, your free training page on *How To Build A Model Train* has received a rising number of visitors. This is a pattern, you recognize it, and you want to investigate. But you can't just magically turn that pattern into a scientific question—you have to figure out where it leads.

You look at the time people are spending on the page, the pages they visit later, where people are arriving to this page from, what links they are clicking, and so on. Data like this is easily accessible through Google Analytics.

You know that the purpose of the free training page is to generate leads. You also know that more people are coming to the page, so you look at your lead flow expecting to see an uptick in lead generation over the last few months.

But, you find, it hasn't changed. Hmm...

Lead conversion rates must have dropped at the same time the traffic started to increase. You look at the data and confirm this is the case.

You then look in Google Analytics to find out where the traffic spike came from. It turns out that the increased traffic has been coming from a news article written by a local newspaper a few months ago. The news article included a link to your website. Good—we're getting closer.

You want to find out how to increase the conversion rate of that traffic, so you start to think about ways you could do that. You know that there are three other free trainings in your company's archives—and a question is suddenly born:

Which free training offer has the highest lead conversion rate for traffic coming from the news article?

You've created a variable (the type of free training). You already have your KPI (the lead conversion rate). Which means you now have a fully formed question.

Now we can begin doing the research.

You open up the news article and read it from top to bottom. You find out what the article really talks about. You read other articles by the same journalist and in the same category. You then open Google Analytics and isolate the news article traffic to see what other pages those people visit.

This is research. It may seem like a rabbit hole, but you will find that the deeper you go, the more you will feel like you understand the situation. You know all the ins-and-outs of the news article traffic. You may even get a good enough understanding of the people coming from the news article that you can guess which free training will generate the most leads. This educated guess is called a **hypothesis**.

STEP THREE: FORM YOUR HYPOTHESIS

The steps of the scientific method get simpler as you go. Coming up with the question is always the hardest part, doing the research is a little easier since you *kind of* know what to look for—and forming a hypothesis is simply a matter of choosing a side.

The hypothesis causes us to view the experiment in the correct context. It helps us pay attention to the right things and draw a line in the sand in terms of our expectations of what will happen. A good hypothesis comes in the form of an answer to your experiment's question. If your question is:

Which free training offer has the highest lead conversion rate?

Then your hypothesis could be:

The free training on How To Build A Model Car will generate the highest lead conversion rate.

The hypothesis is an educated guess, and it is okay if your educated guess ends up being wrong. In the case of **Creative Brainstorm** questions, though, the hypothesis should imply your motivation to run the experiment in the first place. For example, when we ran the Zeigarnik Process Animation experiment at Vivid Labs, our hypothesis was that the animation would increase purchases. If our hypothesis stated that we believed the animation would decrease purchases, then what is the point in running the experiment at all? The hypothesis is an educated guess—it should implicitly suggest that all the brainstorming and research you have done led to the creation of the variants in your experiment.

Your hypothesis draws a line in the sand. It states your position and allows the rest of the scientific method to return an answer in simple terms—either your hypothesis was correct or incorrect. Either result is perfectly fine; a lot of people think if their hypothesis is incorrect, they did something wrong. That is not true. Finding out how things *don't* work is just as valuable as finding out how they *do* work. Both outcomes help you move forward toward the performance improvements you are looking for.

STEP FOUR: CONDUCT
YOUR EXPERIMENT

Note: If you have a brick-and-mortar business, I encourage you to still read through this process, along with the Brick-and-Mortar business section I've added below to help translate these steps into a physical location.

Once you have formed a hypothesis, it is time to plan and launch your split test. These days, running a marketing split test is pretty easy and can cost you nothing. I have used almost every split testing software on the market, and they all get the job done. The one I would recommend when you are just getting started, however, is Google Optimize. It is free and easy to use, and it has nearly every core feature you would find in other split testing software platforms that cost hundreds or thousands of dollars per month[43].

If you are using a marketing tool like ClickFunnels, Samcart, LeadPages, or Unbounce, you will have split testing features already built-in and won't need to use a third-party platform like Google Optimize.

As you begin the creation of your experiment, you will use your split testing tool to duplicate your control and make changes to the variable to create your variant(s). Once you do that, you may also be asked to set up your **goal**.

The goal is your KPI—just under a different name. The platform will walk you through setting up the platform to track goal conversions from new leads to purchases. This involves putting a piece of code into the "header" section of your funnel web pages. If you are not a tech-friendly sort of person, don't be intimidated—the platforms have made this very simple to do and they have plenty of customer support to help you get everything set up properly.

---

43 When you start getting more advanced, you can explore other platforms like Visual Website Optimizer. While these platforms charge for their services, they do have more advanced features and analytics that make it easier for high-traffic websites to run more complex split tests.

The final step to setting up your experiment is to split your traffic—this is known as **traffic allocation**. This means you will send *some* of your funnel traffic to the control (the original page) and the remainder of the traffic will be automatically sent to the variants. In most cases, you will want to split the traffic evenly. So, if you have a control and one variant, you will split the traffic 50/50. If you have a control and three variants, you will split the traffic 25/25/25/25, and so on.

Just before launching your experiment, you will need to test your variants. When making any changes to the copywriting, design, or technical functions of a web page, things can break. It is important to check your variants for mobile responsiveness, typos, design errors, and any technical issues that could arise during the editing process. Once you have done that, and you know your variants are all looking and performing properly, it is time to hit *launch.*

By launching your experiment, you are telling the testing platform to start splitting the traffic between your control and variant(s). This is the final moment before you can sit back and wait for data to come in. At this point, you **cannot** make any further changes to the variants. Any changes you make would require the data to be reset—if you change a variable halfway through an experiment, you would not be able to draw meaningful conclusions. So, before you launch, be sure you have completed all of the necessary steps outlined above.

In a couple of chapters, you will be provided with an exercise and another element of your marketing operating system to ensure this process is followed properly and split tests are properly followed-up and documented.

A Note For Brick-And-Mortar Businesses

If you have a physical location, the steps above may seem irrelevant, but I cannot stress enough how important they are for your own optimization purposes. Once you have formed your hypothesis, you need to create your experiment, but you won't be using software to change your in-store experience. Nor will you be splitting your visitors into two groups as they enter your store. Instead, you will create cohorts.

Cohorts are groups of people who you have decided will have a particular type of experience in your store. For example, if your variable is the product placement in your store window, you can plan for a variant to be a different product layout, or different featured product, in your window. Then you assign certain dates to each cohort of store visitors. For example, you can assign the first two weeks of June to Cohort 1 which will see the existing window display. Then you can assign the second two weeks of June to Cohort 2 which will see the new window display.

Over the course of June, you will have two groups of approximately equal size who will see two different window displays. If you have technology in place to measure foot traffic outside as well as through your door, you can use that as your KPI—that is, you will be testing which window display generates the highest entry rate to your store.

STEP FIVE: ANALYZE YOUR DATA

Neil deGrasse Tyson

Your experiment is complete when you have collected enough data to draw a proper conclusion. The big question most marketers ignore (mostly because they don't know it is important) is *"How much data is enough?"*

Before I get into the answer, it's important to mention **data integrity.** There's a saying in the analysis world: *Garbage in, garbage out.* This means that if you are building an analysis on inaccurate or biased data, your analysis will be inaccurate or biased.

One big cause of unintended bias in experimental data is the **History Effect.** This is a research term that describes the corruption of experimental data due to a unique event occurring. In the window display example we used in the last chapter, if your business was in the USA and you, instead, chose to run your experiment in July, you would have a big spike in visitors on the fourth of July.

This increase wouldn't be attributable to your window display, but it would still show up in your experiment data. Be sure to go back and remove any data that would have been corrupted—in the example above, that would be all data from July 4 (and possibly any corresponding weekend days).

Once you've ensured your data is clean, it's time to start with the analysis. This lies in the realm of statistics, which is normally pretty complicated. Fortunately for you, online testing platforms do all the heavy lifting for you. They crunch the numbers and tell you when the test is complete. But it is still really important to understand what is involved with this number-crunching process, so here's your crash course in statistics:

The field of statistics (or *statistical analysis*) is focused on making predictions. In the case of marketing, those predictions help you know, to a high degree of certainty, whether or not your "winner" is actually a winner, or if it is just in the lead by pure luck. The threshold we use to describe the difference between lucky results and predictable results is called **statistical significance.**

A statistically significant result can tell you to a degree of certainty, usually 95% or 99%, that one of your variants will *continue* to outperform the control, or vice versa. The way we reach statistically significant results is by collecting enough data to be able to make reliable predictions. Generally speaking, the more data you have, the more statistically significant your results will be.

Now here's how your experiment affects the statistics:

The wider the margin of performance between your control and your variant(s) (meaning, if your variant WAY outperforms the control), the less time you will need to run your split test. That is to say, if you are testing the layout of your Landing Page, and your variant outperforms the control by 50%, you won't need to run your experiment very long to reach a reliable result.

Statistical analysis gets to make these predications because of something called a **probability distribution.** Here is an example of a probability distribution for a landing page's conversion rate:

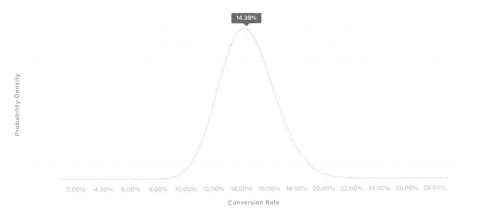

This graph shows, to a level of 95% confidence[44], all of the possible future conversion rates of the landing page. Everything underneath the curved line represents likely outcomes while the space above the line represents unlikely outcomes.

---

44   This means that we can predict, 95 out of 100 times, that the performance of the landing page will fall under the line of the graph.

You will notice that the graph is curved. This is known in statistics as a *normal distribution,* or a **bell curve.** The most likely outcomes are centered around the center, or the average[45], performance of the landing page over the course of the testing period. The wider the bell curve becomes, the less certain we are about making predictions. As the curve gets narrower, there's a higher likelihood of the page performing exactly as expected—in the image above, that would be a 14.39% conversion rate. This doesn't mean that we expect the page to constantly perform at 14.39%—rather, we expect it to perform *around* that rate. Some days will be higher, and some days will be lower.

Let's say we treated the graph above as the control in our experiment and then launched a handful of new variants for the landing page using the headline as the variable. Over the course of the split test, our software would create a graph that looks like this:

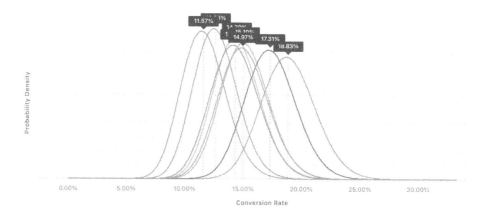

Yes, it's a lot of lines.

But do you see how some curves are positioned to the left and some are positioned to the right? Those are each of the headlines' probability distributions. The curve all the way to the left represents a headline that is predicted to perform quite poorly, whereas the curve all the way to the right is performing best at 18.83%.

With enough data, these curves will become narrower and narrower, and eventually we will be able to compare them. The split testing software you are using does this automatically. Put simply, it compares the likelihood of one curve

---

45   Also known as the *mean*

outperforming the other on a consistent basis. Once the experiment has reached statistical significance[46], you have a winner and a loser.

You can try this out on your own using a statistical significance calculator to find out if an experiment has enough data to determine a winner. My favorite calculator is on Visual Website Optimizer's website (www.vwo.com) under the Resources tab. I recommend trying it out so you can get a feel for what kind of data would be considered statistically significant.

A/B Split Test Significance Calculator

Built with ♥ for testing, optimization, UX, CRO, and design teams.

	Number of Visitors	Number of Conversions
Control	1000	50
Variation	1000	200

CALCULATE SIGNIFICANCE

P-Value	Significant?
0	Yes!

The P-Value is **0** Hence, your results are statistically significant!

It's free to use. Just type in your experiment data and it will spit out a simple answer to let you know if your experiment is complete or if you need to collect more data. If you are using any kind of software for your split testing, like Google Optimize, Visual Website Optimizer, or ClickFunnels, you'll be given this information within the platform itself—no calculator needed.

---

46 Keep in mind that this is an oversimplified version of the full statistical analysis that occurs. You don't need to become a math genius and understand everything about this in order to run a split test.

Inconclusive Split Tests

In some cases, your experiment will end up running too long to be practical. This can happen for two reasons.

First, if your control and variant(s) are performing almost identically, it is difficult to achieve statistical significance. This is because those bell curves that we saw above would be almost directly on top of one another. The statistics wouldn't be able to determine the likelihood of one curve outperforming the other(s) 95% of the time, which means you would have to build up a *ton* of data in order to get a meaningful result. In these cases, it is better to end the experiment and plan another one. The experiment's conclusion, in this case, would be that the results were inconclusive due to insufficient data.

Second, if you don't have enough time to collect the necessary data (such as low website traffic), your experiment will just keep going and going, never leading to an actionable conclusion. In these cases, you have two options. You can either end the experiment, as mentioned above, or you can find a way to increase your traffic. This would call for additional advertising budget, a new campaign, a split test one step before the step you are currently testing, or some other way to increase the number of people arriving to the funnel step you want to improve.

Planning Ahead

There are ways to estimate the amount of time an experiment will take. Keep in mind that only time will tell, but it is possible to use a calculator to predict how long your test needs to reach a 95% level of confidence.

Visual Website Optimizer's website (www.vwo.com) provides another calculator for this. You can find it, again, in the Resources tab on their website.

Average number of daily visitors who will participate in the test (control + variation)	200
Estimated existing conversion rate (%)	30 %
Minimum improvement in conversion rate you want to detect (%)	20 %
Number of variations/combinations (including control)	6

CALCULATE TEST DURATION

This calculator will ask for some basic information:

1. The average number of visitors you are expecting to arrive on the funnel step you are testing
2. The existing KPI of your control
3. The minimum improvement you want to detect (keep this at the default 20% when you are just getting started)
4. The number of variants, including the control, in your split test

Use this calculator if you are concerned about your split test taking too long. If you find that your test is estimated to take too long, try decreasing the number of variants you are using (if you have more than one). The more variants you have, the longer the test is likely to take.

You can also see how an increase in traffic affects your test duration. Although, as I mentioned above, that would mean you have to put resources into making that increase happen, whether through a new campaign, further testing upstream in your funnel, or increasing your ad budget.

The final thing you can do to decrease your estimated test duration is to increase the *minimum improvement you want to detect* (item #3 in the calculator). I don't recommend this if you are just getting started because it puts your experiment at risk if your variants and control perform too similarly. That being said, increasing that number will decrease the sensitivity of your test, which will pull down the estimated duration. This doesn't affect the statistical significance of any results you do get, but it does increase the risk that a "close tie" between your variants and control will render your experiment inconclusive. Use this tactic at your own risk.

Once You Receive Conclusive Data

As soon as your split test reaches a 95% level of statistical significance (this 95% level is built-in on most testing platforms, so you likely won't have to worry about it), you can move on to the final step of the scientific method: drawing your conclusions.

STEP SIX: AND THE WINNER IS...

If they passed the analysis stage, your split test results will be as clear as day. You will have one variant, or your control, that outperformed by a large enough margin to be predictable. This is a great achievement!

You will be ready, at this point, to de-activate all of the losing variants and/or the control, leaving 100% of the funnel step traffic to be sent to the winner. This means that if you were testing four headlines against one another (including the control), instead of 25% of all funnel step visitors seeing the winning headline, now 100% of them will see it. This will give you an instant boost in performance.

It is still important at this point to complete the full scientific method—that is, documenting your conclusions. This is a step that gets skipped a lot, too. People get so excited about having a winner that they launch the winning variant to 100% of visitors and then *forget to finish the test.*

This final step is what allows your split test to benefit your business for years to come. By documenting your conclusions, you can build up a library of marketing best-practices that new team members can refer to when building funnel steps, writing emails, or creating any other type of marketing asset.

Let's say that one of your split tests found that a particular type of landing page layout outperformed any other layout you have tried. Wouldn't you want to use that layout as the *starting point* for any future landing pages your company designs? Of course! Documenting your conclusions allows you to do this. It avoids having to reinvent the wheel every time you need to create a new piece of marketing material.

We accomplish this goal in your marketing operating system by saving your conclusions in a **Split Test Briefing.** Your Split Test Briefing is a document that outlines the process of your split test, from question to conclusion. It also helps you keep track of your data and estimate timelines. If you report on marketing progress to anyone in your organization, it is easily printable and savable as a PDF that you can email to your manager or CMO.

Exercise: Create Your Split Test Briefing

When you are ready to plan and launch your first split test using the steps you have just learned, it is time to create your Split Test Briefing. Go to **heydanrussell.com/snakeoil** and you can get the Split Test Briefing template for free. Be sure to complete the document carefully and spend the necessary time to do your research. With this tool in hand, you will be able to plan and launch split tests with confidence.

Assignment: Schedule Your Split Test Sprints

This is the final step of installing your marketing operating system. Split Test Sprints are short, regularly held meetings (or, if you are a solo founder, spots on your calendar) during which you review your campaign and funnel performance, use the Funnel Grid to ask intelligent "what-if" questions, review active split tests, and plan new split tests.

Split Test Sprints should be held weekly and last no longer than 60 minutes. When held at this frequency, you can rely on a regular weekly checkpoint on your marketing operations **without** getting side-tracked by new campaign ideas (if this happens, you need to schedule a new Campaign Creation Meeting).

You can find an agenda for your Split Test Sprints at **heydanrussell.com/ snakeoil**

Your marketing performance changes more often than almost anything in business. You *must* keep a close eye on your numbers and find new ways to fix bottlenecks as soon as they pop up. That's what the Split Test Sprints are for. You will find, as time passes, that these meetings become part of your weekly cadence as a company. As a result, you will be more agile in your response to new bottlenecks and more proactive in finding creative ways to build an even better sales funnel.

THE NEUROTACTIC LIBRARY

"The difference between screwing around and science is writing it down."

Adam Savage

When I was getting started with split testing, one of the hardest parts was figuring out what to test. Before I learned all of this, the hypothesis and research stages always seemed random to me. Like I was expected to pull a split test out of a hat and *hope* it would work.

It usually didn't.

Random testing isn't a strategy. It's a gamble—and I learned that the hard way. Over time, though, I began to learn more about neuroscience, behavioral economics, and psychology. I eventually started to see connections between the way our brains work and the way we buy things.

I began translating this complicated research into practical and ethical marketing principles that could be tested in a marketing campaign or funnel. This became known as my **Creative Brainstorming** approach that we spoke about a few chapters ago. What emerged from hundreds of these Creative Brainstorms was a library of marketing "NeuroTactics" supported by real results and well-established brain science research.

That library is contained in the chapters that follow. Each NeuroTactic contains a description of a mental pattern that all human beings exhibit. Depending on the NeuroTactic's marketing application, it will be categorized into one of five buckets: Desire, Routing, Emotion, Attention, or Memory. Short descriptions have been provided for each of these categories so you know how best to use the NeuroTactics within. That being said, there's nothing stopping you from finding creative applications of these principles! I hope they inspire you to create your own innovative split tests and build powerful marketing campaigns for your own business.

This is also not an exhaustive list of NeuroTactics—there are other people and companies out there collecting marketing-related brain research. My two favorites are Cognitive Lode (www.coglode.com) and The Decision Lab (www. thedecisionlab.com). Both of these companies are excellent sources of marketing-related research, and they have amazing resources on their websites that you can use in addition to the library below.

⚮ DESIRE

This category of NeuroTactics is designed to activate the "buy button" in our brains known as the ventro-medial prefrontal cortex (vmPFC). These Neuro Tactics have been extensively tested in fields from psychology to behavioral economics. **They are ideal to use when you're trying to improve the conversion rates of your sales funnel.**

Anchoring[47]

When faced with a decision, our brains look for information in all kinds of places to determine whether we are facing a good choice or a bad one. In the case of judging prices, we will subconsciously refer to the last numbers in our short-term memory to make our judgment.

Setting quantifiable anchors in the short-term memory of a prospect will cause them to consider not just the price of your product or service, but also how that price compares to the anchor. That comparison will be used to judge whether your price is reasonable. Setting an MSRP is an example of anchoring in the retail and e-commerce industry. Even though nobody ever pays the MSRP, this price is still taken into consideration during the buying process.

If you are running a service business, you can use competitor pricing or industry average pricing in order to provide an anchor for the price of your own services. If you charge a premium and avoid running discounts or keeping prices low (such as a luxury concierge service), anchoring will be difficult (and possibly off-brand) for you.

---

47 Sugden, Robert, et al. "Not All Anchors Are Created Equal." Journal of Economic Psychology, vol. 39, 2013, pp. 21–31., doi:10.1016/j.joep.2013.06.008.

Certainty[48]

Certainty is valued highly, and we will pay a premium for it, when outcomes are unknown and potentially negative.

If your customers are taking a risk in buying your product, go out of your way to add more certainty to the process. Explain the steps that follow a transaction, how they will access and use their product, and try to answer questions ahead of time with FAQ sections. This will create more certainty around their decision to buy from you.

Another way to take advantage of this effect is to reinforce steps that have already been taken by your customer. This can take the form of a congratulatory video after completing an important milestone, a checklist containing steps completed thus far, or a breadcrumb navigation to provide context of where in your website a visitor is. This strategy pairs nicely with the *Zeigarnik Effect*.

This effect is different from, but is not the opposite to, the *Motivating Uncertainty Effect*. The *Certainty Effect* takes hold when we use certainty to create an emotional "security blanket" while facing a risky situation; the *Motivating Uncertainty Effect* takes hold when we use uncertainty to increase motivation in a less risk-prone scenario.

Commitment Expansion[49]

In a research study involving 88 people at a charity event, a group of people was asked to wear a badge for the evening in support of a charitable cause. At the end of the evening, the researchers added up how much each guest had donated. The group of people wearing the badges ended up donating more, on average, than those who had not worn the badges.

Commitment Expansion occurs when one small, seemingly benign decision, such as wearing a simple badge, can multiply into a larger and more important decision. In many cases, there is a core belief behind both decisions which drives this expansion. In the case of the research study above, that core belief was that the charity was a cause worthy of donating money to. When we experience Com-

---

48   Tversky, A, and D Kahneman. "The Framing of Decisions and the Psychology of Choice." Science, vol. 211, no. 4481, 1981, pp. 453–458., doi:10.1126/science.7455683.

49   Burger, Jerry M. "The Foot-in-the-Door Compliance Procedure: A Multiple-Process Analysis and Review." Personality and Social Psychology Review, vol. 3, no. 4, 1999, pp. 303–325., doi:10.1207/s15327957pspr0304_2.

mitment Expansion, the smaller decision ends up making the larger decision feel easier and more organic than if the smaller decision hadn't been made.

Decide what your large decision is—whether that's attending a consultation, buying your product, or something else in your customer journey. Then reverse-engineer your way backward to a small, simple step someone can take toward that larger decision. Try to identify a core belief that both decisions are based on and focus on reinforcing that core belief in the interim time between the small and large decisions.

Endowed Progress Effect[50]

In a study of 300 people visiting a car wash, researchers found that using a rewards card affected how often patrons returned to the car wash. The control group of 150 car wash patrons were given a normal rewards card with 8 stamp spots—every time you visit the business, you receive a stamp. The promise to the patrons was that they would receive a free car wash if they returned to the car wash 8 times to receive 8 stamps. The other 150 patrons received the same card, but instead of 8 empty stamp spots, they received cards with 10 stamp spots and 2 spots already stamped as a "favor."

Despite the fact that both groups of 150 people required 8 stamps to claim their free car wash, the second group (with the 10 stamp spots and 2 free stamps) came back more often to redeem their free car wash. In fact, their redemption rate was almost *twice* that of the group who didn't receive the two free stamps. The head start given by the two free stamps triggered the *Endowed Progress Effect*, causing the second group to feel more motivated to finish getting the rest of the stamps.

The Endowed Progress Effect states that we have a higher chance of achieving a goal that we have a head start toward, especially when there's a reward for achieving the goal.

The most direct applications of the Endowed Progress Effect are web page progress bars with 20-30% head starts, sign-up bonuses (such as points when you sign up for a new credit card), "new customer boosts" in a loyalty program, and bonuses upon signing up for an affiliate program. Any kind of head start that encourages a

---

50   Nunes, Joseph C., and Xavier Dreze. "The Endowed Progress Effect: How Artificial Advancement Increases Effort." PsycEXTRA Dataset, 2006, doi:10.1037/e621442012-134.

customer or partner to achieve a certain goal, such as coming back to a car wash a certain number of times, can be used to trigger the Endowed Progress Effect.

Endowment Effect[51]

When we feel a sense of ownership around something, we give it a higher value than if we didn't own it. In an experiment with coffee mugs and chocolate, study participants showed a higher preference to keep an item they were previously given rather than trade it for another item of similar monetary value.

This effect is caused by a difference between the price we are willing to pay for an item and the price we are willing to accept to part with it. Free trials make use of this effect to a great degree by giving prospective customers a sense of ownership over a product before they have paid to acquire it. Thus, when the trial is over, their "selling price" for the item has become higher than what you are charging for it, which causes their willingness to pay a higher price to increase.

To put this effect to work in your marketing, try to think of creative ways of getting your customers involved with your product prior to the purchase. This could be a free trial, test drive, or sample. If you operate a service business, this could be a discovery period with a customized deliverable, such as a tailored action plan. Having ownership over this deliverable asset will trigger the Endowment Effect and increase the perceived value of your service through a heightened sense of ownership and control.

Framing Effect[52]

The presentation of a fact affects our interpretation of how important or relevant the fact is. In an experiment testing the effect of packaging of ground beef, shoppers rated beef as higher quality when it was displayed as "75% lean" versus "25% fat," even though the two facts communicate the same information.

Take a close look at the facts and features you are using in your marketing. What frame is "around" the data you are sharing, and how is that construed by your prospects? It may benefit you to change the frame and thus change the perception that your data is creating about your brand.

---

51   Knetsch, Jack L. "The Endowment Effect and Evidence of Nonreversible Indifference Curves." *Choices, Values, and Frames*, 2000, pp. 171–179., doi:10.1017/cbo9780511803475.010.

52   Tversky, A, and D Kahneman. "The Framing of Decisions and the Psychology of Choice." Science, vol. 211, no. 4481, 1981, pp. 453–458., doi:10.1126/science.7455683.

This NeuroTactic can also be applied to marketing messages beyond just data points like prices or the ground beef example above. If, for example, you are a consultant trying to describe the value of your services, you have the option to appeal to the pain you relieve or the pleasure you create. For example, you can focus your message on the amount of money you will *save* your client—or you can focus on the amount of money you will *make* your client. Both communicate the same thing—value creation—but each message appeals to a very different audience with different priorities.

Motivating Uncertainty Effect[53]

In situations where a positive result is uncertain, like when we know there's a possibility for a reward or some other "win," like a lottery, we have a higher motivation to trust and engage with the process. When someone finds themselves in one of these scenarios, they'll go out of their way or pay a premium for uncertainty *rather than* certainty.

Uncertainty can be used to your advantage in marketing by creating a sense of curiosity and mystery around an end result, reward, sweepstakes, giveaway, or trial. Try to incorporate a level of uncertain rewards, based on customer engagement, purchase history, or some other metric, into your customer journey.

Brand trust is a requirement in order to effectively trigger the Motivating Uncertainty Effect. People trust a lottery since it's an established organization and heavily regulated. Try to ensure you have a deep level of trust with your audience before engaging this NeuroTactic.

Prospect Theory[54]

If you were given $10 by a random stranger on the street, you would probably feel good. But if someone ran up to you a few seconds later and stole the $10 bill out of your hand, you would feel worse off than you did before you received the $10 in the first place, even though you are no worse off. This is called *Prospect Theory*.

---

53 Shen, Luxi, et al. "The Motivating-Uncertainty Effect: Uncertainty Increases Resource Investment in the Process of Reward Pursuit." *Journal of Consumer Research*, vol. 41, no. 5, 2015, pp. 1301–1315., doi:10.1086/679418.
54 Kahneman, Daniel, and Amos Tversky. "Prospect Theory. an Analysis of Decision Making under Risk." 1977, doi:10.21236/ada045771.

We feel more pain from a loss than we feel from a gain of equal value. In fact, we take more risks to avoid pain than we do to achieve an equal gain. And as we gain more, we value each of the same types of gain less and less (this is called *Diminishing Marginal Utility*). This behavior affects everything from our purchasing decisions to our relationships.

Consider bundling together the "painful" elements of your product. Offer annual subscriptions instead of monthly or bundle services together that you know would otherwise be purchased separately. When planning your customer journey, try to add time between benefits, such as limiting the use of your product to a certain frequency or spreading out rewards in your loyalty program.

Reciprocity[55]

In his marketing book *Influence,* Robert Cialdini recounted the story of the financial struggles of the Hare Krishna religion in the 1960s. In an effort to raise donations, the Hare Krishnas began going to airports to ask for contributions from travelers. Cialdini says that he visited multiple airports to see this happen, and every time, the same thing happened.

Members of Hare Krishna would give small gifts to passersby, from flowers to books. These bystanders often didn't know what Hare Krishna was, much less whether it was a cause they agreed with. Yet, when they received this gift, the "rule of reciprocation" (as Cialdini calls it) took over and they reached into their pocket to give the Hare Krishna member some money, or at the very least stopped to listen.

One of the most deeply rooted human behaviors is the return of kindness received. This is known as *reciprocity*. When we receive kindness from others, we are wired to return it in some form in the future. Even chimpanzees demonstrate the same behavior.

Your initial exchanges with prospects and customers will set the tone for their level of reciprocity. Something as simple as a free giveaway can trigger the desire to return a favor in the future. Try to think about creative ways you can give to your audience in a way that will cause them to return the favor in the form of more attention or even a purchase.

---

55 Jacob, C., Gueguen, N. & Boulbry, G. (2015). Effect of an unexpected small favor on compliance with a survey request. Journal of Business Research, 68-56-59.

Scarcity[56]

The more limited something is, the more we desire it. This is a core economic pillar and the basis of supply and demand. If the demand for a product stays the same and supply decreases, the price increases.

This economic application is just one example of how scarcity can be applied in the marketing world. There are four primary ways to incorporate scarcity into your marketing and products: time, exclusivity, and availability.

Limited-time offers are one way to incorporate time scarcity into your promotions (this is a tried-and-true strategy of direct response marketing). Limited edition or limited quantity versions of products are one way of fostering scarcity in availability, and VIP clubs are using scarcity of access (exclusivity) as a way to boost membership.

Social Proof[57]

Our behaviors are constantly influenced by the behavior of others. When we are in a new environment or faced with a new decision, we look around toward other people for a clue as to what the "right" behavior or decision is. In marketing, this is known as *Social Proof*.

Social proof comes in many forms, but the most popular and well-known form is the testimonial. Whether written or in a multimedia format, a testimonial shows prospects that your product or service is not risky. The more testimonials you have, the more persuasive your argument is.

There are many other forms of social proof beyond the testimonial. Any situation in which a large group of people is featuring an endorsement of a particular product, service, movement, or brand, social proof is at work.

Specificity[58]

Increasing specificity leads to "enhanced perceptions" about an offer being made to a customer. The more specific the offer, the more likely a consumer is to trust the message and the messenger.

---

56 Bandura & Menlove (1968). Factors determining vicarious extinction through symbolic modeling. Journal of Personality and Social Psychology.
57 Bandura & Menlove (1968). Factors determining vicarious extinction through symbolic modeling. Journal of Personality and Social Psychology.
58 "Roberson, Q.M., Collins, C.J. & Oreg, S. The Effects Of Recruitment Message Specificity On Applicant Attraction To Organizations. J Bus Psychol 19, 319–339 (2005). https://doi.

Generally speaking, specificity leads to clarity. Clarity leads to trust, and trust is the precursor to making a decision to move forward. By establishing specificity, you are painting a clearer picture in the mind of your prospect by establishing clear expectations of what they will receive or experience.

To apply specificity to your marketing, take a look at the claims, benefits, and features that you are sharing. How can you make them clearer and more specific? Also take a close look at your FAQ section and purchase/registration instructions. How can they be as specific as possible so your prospects and customers have more clarity around what they are getting? Adding clarity to your customer's experience, no matter what stage they are at, will lead to higher conversion rates.

org/10.1007/s10869-004-2231-1
https://link.springer.com/article/10.1007/s10869-004-2231-1"

ROUTING

Routing is the second category of NeuroTactics we'll review. This is the process of creating an experience that feels personalized or otherwise "fitting" to the individual. When we feel that something has been created or customized just for us or is the perfect match for what we're looking for, we have a higher interest in engaging with it. The NeuroTactics in this category can create this interest for your audience if used properly.

Attractiveness Effect[59]

When we are choosing between two similar options, we will choose the one with the superior value. Although this sounds like an obvious behavior, the consequences are important.

If you have a single product option, your customers' brains will search for something to compare that product to and find nothing (eventually they will start looking for your competitors as the basis of comparison). By adding a second inferior option next to your product, conversions will likely rise due to the presence of a comparable option.

Compromise Effect[60]

We prefer to make compromises than take risks on extreme options. Given three options for a product choice, we will opt for the middle option as a compromise between price and performance.

---

59 "The Importance of Irrelevant Alternatives." The Economist, The Economist Newspaper, 22 May 2009, www.economist.com/democracy-in-america/2009/05/22/the-importance-of-irrelevant-alternatives.

60 "Simonson (1989). Choice Based on Reasons: The Case of Attraction and Compromise Effects. Journal of Consumer Research, Volume 16, Issue 2, 158–174.
    Wernerfelt (1995). A Rational Reconstruction of the Compromise Effect: Using Market Data to Infer Utilities. The Journal of Consumer Research, Vol. 21, No. 4., 627-633."

If you have the capability of having three product options, add a lower-priced option and a higher-priced option adjacent (on both sides) to your primary product. This will help contextualize your customers' options and focus their attention on the best-value option in the middle.

Default Effect[61]

A default option is one that is pre-selected or pre-chosen for us. Our brains love to make mental shortcuts to save energy. Defaults are the perfect moment for our brains to kick back and let someone else "do the deciding" for us.

You can see defaults at work in online opt-in forms, organ donor applications, and re-purchase options in food delivery apps. The default effect carries an enormous weight in our decision-making process. Defaults can be incorporated into your customer buying journey in many ways, from Facebook lead gen ads that auto-fill contact information to email marketing opt-in checkboxes. Keep in mind, though, that it's important to keep your recommended defaults balanced. Avoid setting default options that don't feel natural to your customers—otherwise, they will stop in their tracks.

Choice Limitation[62]

In an experiment with fruit jams at a supermarket, shoppers had a higher purchase rate of jam jars when there was a smaller selection of jams on a table rather than a large variety. When we have too many options to choose from, we experience overwhelm and disengage—in other words, we *choose not to choose*.

Limiting the choices someone has during the purchasing experience will avoid overwhelming them with options. If you have a variety of different product options to choose from (such as customizing a new computer), separate the purchasing process into multiple steps focused on one category of options at a time rather than offering all of the options at once.

61 Johnson, E. J. & Goldstein, D. (2003). Medicine: Do defaults save lives? Science 302 (5649)
62 Chernev, Bockenholt & Goodman (2015). Choice overload: A conceptual review and meta-analysis. Journal of Consumer Psychology, 25(2), 333-358.

Risk Aversion[63]

We avoid uncertainty in all areas of life, and we're willing to pay a premium to avoid it. Your customers stick to what they know and, when asked to venture outside their past experience, they will avoid it or seek ways of reducing the risk of the venture.

Over the course of selling your products or services, your customers will inevitably reach the point where they feel they are venturing into the unknown. This feeling could be caused by past experience (such as being burned by a similar company in the past), parting with money, or something else entirely.

It's critical to address this feeling by providing risk-averting features of your product or marketing campaign. Examples of such features are money-back guarantees, customer support areas, 24/7 live chat, and bonus-stacking. A well-formed guarantee, however, is the most powerful risk-reversal feature you can include in your marketing, so be sure to include one if at all possible.

Sunk Cost Bias[64]

Even in the cutthroat world of finance, it is difficult to resist our temptation to hold on to bad investments, even when it is in our interest to sell. Stock traders and stockyard workers all have this experience, which is known as *Sunk Cost Bias*. We tend to keep track of the investments we've made into certain products and projects, and when the time comes to admit defeat, we tend to keep moving forward in order to see that investment bear fruit—even if there's a decreasing chance of that happening.

Sunk cost bias applies to both money and time. The lawyer resists giving up on a big case because she remembers all the sleepless nights, while the entrepreneur resists giving up on a new marketing campaign because she remembers the thousands of dollars she invested.

Your prospects and customers have invested time and money into achieving a certain result. They will have a higher willingness to continue investing to achieve that result than switching to a new alternative prospect, but they must be reminded of the investment (or "sunk cost") along the way in order to realize how far they have come.

---

63   Barsky et al. (1997). Preference parameters and behavioral heterogeneity. Quarterly Journal of Economics.

64   Arkes, H.R. & Blumer, C. (1985). The psychology of sunk cost. Organizational behavior and human decision processes, 35(1), 124-140

Be careful with the ethics surrounding this NeuroTactic; although it is powerful, it should not be used to keep customers on a "hamster wheel" by convincing them to continue pursuing a goal that you know is unlikely to be achieved.

⟨ EMOTION

Emotional engagement is at the core of great marketing campaigns and customer journeys. I encourage you to use these NeuroTactics for inspiration in planning not only your split tests, but also your customer support experiences, your product development efforts, and your marketing campaigns.

Autonomy Bias[65]

In a 2011 study involving an exercise program, study participants who had the ability to choose their exercise regimen reported a higher satisfaction level than those who were randomly assigned a regimen.

This pattern echoes throughout many studies in which people are generally happier and more satisfied when they have control over their surroundings. No matter what is being decided, the mere existence of a choice increases a person's satisfaction. The existence of a choice means a person has autonomy, and the existence of autonomy gives a person confidence that they are in control.

Research shows that people use their autonomy more when making discretionary purchases versus practical purchases. For example, consumers will exercise their rights to customize a new car more readily than they will spend time on what types of pens are stocked in their office.

With this in mind, consider how you can add more levels of control to your customer journey. As you hand more autonomy to your audience, they will have a higher level of commitment to seeing the process through. Their excitement around purchasing may be higher and they'll be more motivated to follow through with a purchase.

---

65 Botti & McGill (2011). The locus of choice: Personal causality and satisfaction with hedonic and utilitarian decisions. Journal of Consumer Research

IKEA Effect[66]

When we play a part in the creation of a product, we create an emotional attachment to it and will pay a premium for it. Whether it is a piece of IKEA furniture or an upgrade to our car, our own involvement in the assembly of an item connects us deeply to that item.

Consider possible ways of involving your customers in the assembly of your product or provisioning of your service. Involving them in the process, if it fits your business model, will allow you to demand a premium price. In some cases, this may even save you money, as IKEA does by avoiding the need to ship fully built sofas or to have their employees assemble furniture.

Lucky Loyalty Effect[67]

The more someone spends with your brand, the more they feel entitled to a higher chance of receiving a random reward. If you have a loyalty program that gives away something for free every month, your most loyal customers, regardless of the fact that all of your customers are in the running to win, believe they have an advantage.

This behavior is called the *Lucky Loyalty Effect*. When we spend more time and money with a company, we believe we will get preferential treatment. This belief is further supported through loyalty programs and great customer service. But when we are entered into an uncertain situation in which we have an equal chance of winning something as every other customer, we will think that we have the upper hand.

Even though it's an irrational belief, reinforcing it is important to building customer loyalty. This tactic can be used to increase the completion of otherwise mundane or boring tasks, such as training programs. By adding uncertain, or even random, rewards for those who have already demonstrated engagement and loyalty, the completion rate of a particular task will likely increase.

---

66   Norton, Mochon, & Ariely (2011). The 'IKEA Effect': When labor leads to love. Harvard Business School Marketing Unit Working Paper, 11-091
67   Reczek, Haws, & Summers (2014) Lucky Loyalty: The Effect of Consumer Effort on Predictions of Randomly Determined Marketing Outcomes, Journal of Consumer Research

Mere Exposure Effect[68]

The more often we encounter a brand, item, or person, the more likely we are to develop a liking. Whether it is a company, a colleague, or a car, if we spend more time with something or someone, our minds become more familiar. This familiarity leads to trust, which then leads to liking.

The more often someone is exposed to your brand, whether it is a billboard or social media ad, the more familiar they will become with it. Over time, with enough exposure, they will have a higher and higher likelihood of engaging with you. Be careful not to annoy them, however. Too high of an ad frequency can lead to outright dismissal of your brand.

Mood-Congruent Memory Bias[69]

Our moods determine the memories that are most easily retrievable in a given moment. If you are sitting in traffic, your brain is subtly recalling other moments that you've been stuck in traffic. But, while your brain is performing that recall in order to guide your decisions in the present moment, it's also retrieving the mood you were feeling at those past times as well, which was likely frustration or anxiety around being late. Memories become more easily retrievable—along with the associated feelings—by your state of *being* in a certain mood.

As psychology website Alley Dog puts it, "For instance, it is a holiday and you are feeling happy and relaxed. That mood by itself can evoke other memories of holidays, fun times, family get-togethers, etc... Anything that shares the current mood. Likewise, something bad happens in your life. This brings up similar bad memories of negative events and can plunge a person into a spiral of despair. Although the actual process behind this is not well understood, it is very common."

This is why people will become more open to transformative work 30 minutes into a personal growth coaching session than at the outset. They have been brought into the right mood by going through a series of visualizations.

---

68   "Zajonc, Robert B. (1968). ""Attitudinal Effects Of Mere Exposure"". Journal of
     Personality and Social Psychology.
     Bornstein, Robert F. (1989). ""Exposure and affect: Overview and meta-analysis of research,
     1968-1987"". Psychological Bulletin."
69   Howe ML, Malone C. Mood-congruent true and false memory: effects of depression.
     Memory. 2011 Feb;19(2):192-201. doi: 10.1080/09658211.2010.544073. Epub 2011 Feb
     2. PMID: 21294037.

If you find yourself in the situation of having to reach an audience who is either dismissive of your product or has some kind of resistance to paying close attention to you, focus first on reminding them of positive memories and thoughts. This will help lift them into a place of *feeling* more positive, which can contribute to a more positive outlook toward you.

Present Bias[70]

We often make decisions that are good for us in the short run, but against our long-term goals. This "present bias" appears when you are walking by a favorite store, deciding what to eat, or trying to break a habit.

The present bias can be ethically applied to businesses by giving customers the option to pre-purchase a product or service that they know will be beneficial in the long run, or to offer products that have faster turnaround or quicker delivery times. Be careful, though—improper use of this bias would be to encourage destructive behavior at the cost of a customer's long-term goals.

Surprise Effect[71]

A group of restaurant patrons was given free desserts and then broken into two groups. One of those groups was given an explanation as to why they received the dessert, and the other group was given no explanation. The former group (which received the explanation) experienced a higher level of enjoyment than the other group.

When we receive an unexpected and personal gesture from a company or person, we feel appreciated and valued. When we receive an explanation of why we received the gesture, our delight increases even more.

When you are crafting your customer experience, it is critical to not only surprise your prospects and customers with gestures of kindness, but also reaffirm why they are receiving it. Keep in mind not to do this too often, however, as the effect will eventually wear off if experienced too frequently.

---

70   Van Epps et al. (2016). Advance ordering for healthier eating? Journal of Marketing Research

71   Gyung Kim & Mattila (2013). Does a surprise strategy need words? The effect of explanations... on delight & expectations. Journal of Services Marketing

⊛ ATTENTION

Capturing your audience's attention is the job of your marketing campaign, but maintaining that attention is the job of the sales funnel. As a result, it's important to incorporate attention-*keeping* techniques across your entire customer journey, from the first impression to the last transaction. Attention NeuroTactics are designed to help you cut through the noise of news feeds and other channels so you can keep your audience focused on you.

Attentional Bias[72]

People tend to pay closer attention to, and more easily notice, sensory cues that align with their recurring thoughts at the time. For example, someone who is hungry will have a higher tendency to notice restaurants.

Ask yourself what your customer's recurring thoughts are (what they are most familiar with and what they think about regularly) at the moment they could pay attention to you. How can you incorporate those thoughts into your marketing materials, from your imagery to your copywriting? Be sure to maintain an ethical approach to this strategy and only focus on positive recurring thoughts rather than negative recurring thoughts, such as anxiety or depression. Focusing on these negative thoughts can lead to dangerous territory, both ethically and legally.

Authority Bias[73]

In an experiment aimed at finding out how many people would pay the parking ticket of a random stranger, 33% of people gave the money when asked

---

72   Bar-Haim, Yair; Lamy, Dominique; Pergamin, Lee; Bakermans-Kranenburg, Marian J.; van IJzendoorn, Marinus H. (2007). "Threat-related attentional bias in anxious and nonanxious individuals: A meta-analytic study". Psychological Bulletin. 133 (1): 1–24.
73   Bickman, L (1974). The social power of uniform. Journal of Applied Social Psychology 4, 47-61.

by a fellow civilian whereas 89% of people gave the money when asked by a police officer.

We have a higher likelihood of paying attention to, and trusting, a figure of authority than someone with relatively little authority. This is known as *Authority Bias*. Adding authoritative elements to your marketing materials such as endorsements, certifications, and expert testimonials will boost the level of trust that prospects have in your brand.

An important difference between Authority Bias and Social Proof is that Authority Bias deals exclusively with people and companies which are well-known and well-respected. Social Proof, on the other hand, deals with the "everyman" who is in the same position, or a similar position, as the person viewing the campaign or funnel.

Baader-Meinhof Phenomenon[74]

This is the effect felt when, upon encountering a new person, place, or thing, we seem to notice it with a higher frequency than before it was noticed. This is also known as the "Red Car Syndrome" due to a high number of people, during the car buying process, tending to notice their intended car on the road more frequently.

Practically and ethically applied to marketing strategy, the Baader-Meinhof Phenomenon gives us the ability to increase the frequency of attention generated toward your product or brand after a customer learns about it for the first time. This is useful in retargeting ads—in the case of retargeting, you can control (and in many ways supercharge) this effect by guaranteeing that a group of people who have engaged with your brand at least once begin to notice you more frequently, which leads to a higher level of familiarity and trust (see *Mere Exposure Effect* for a complementary NeuroTactic).

Category Size Bias[75]

In an experiment with 15 lottery balls, researchers painted 11 of the balls red and asked study participants which ball they would bet on. Participants over-

---

74   Zwicky, Arnold. "Just Between Dr. Language and I." Language Log: Just between Dr. Language and I, University of Pennsylvania, itre.cis.upenn.edu/~myl/languagelog/archives/002386.html.

75   Isaac & Brough (2014). Judging a Part by the Size of Its Whole: The Category Size Bias in Probability Judgments.

whelmingly chose the painted balls—even though each ball had an equal likelihood of winning. This is known as *Category Size Bias*.

This bias causes us to believe that an option classified into a large category is superior to an option classified into a smaller category. In addition, we tend to believe that options within large categories "take on" on the characteristics of the category itself. In reality, neither belief is rooted in fact.

When providing options to your customers, use category sizes to direct their attention to the products you would like to sell most. Avoid using too many categories (this will lead to choice overwhelm) and choose your categories based on criteria that are relevant to your brand or customer (for example, if you are selling baseball hats, organize them by team or material rather than color).

Confirmation Bias[76]

We tend to seek out, interpret, and remember things that confirm our existing beliefs rather than things that contradict our beliefs. We feel better when our beliefs are supported than when they are challenged, so we naturally (and subconsciously) put ourselves in the situation of re-affirming our worldview at every possible chance we get.

If your product or service deals in an industry or with a topic that is emotionally charged or sensitive, this effect will be in full gear with your prospects and customers. Strongly state your position in the market and communicate what you believe. You will find that customers who agree with you will flock toward you.

Context Effect[77]

Our brains are pattern-recognition engines. They seek to fill in gaps in our sensory experiences, such as a missing word in a sentence, as well as gaps in our emotional experiences, such as when we return to a familiar place or see someone we know. In the latter situation, our memories contribute to the foundation upon which we build our emotional state. We refer to past experiences to determine how to feel and how to behave.

---

76 McClure, Li, Tomlin, Cypert, Montague & Montague (2004). Neural correlates of behavioral preference for culturally familiar drinks. Neuron, 44(2), 379-387.

77 Rooderkerk, Robert P; Van Heerde, Harald J; Bijmolt, Tammo H.A (1 August 2011). "Incorporating Context Effects Into a Choice Model". Journal of Marketing Research. 48 (4): 767–780.

Your customers are regularly returning to familiar environments that you create; email broadcasts, text messages, brick and mortar locations, meeting rooms, and video conferences are just a few. Make these environments memorable in order to reinforce brand experiences that are rooted in trust and stability.

Feedback Loops[78]

The government of Garden Grove, California installed five radar speed signs at five separate locations in which drivers routinely drove too fast. The sign would flash a bright light and display a driver's speed if they were 5MPH or more above the limit. After these signs were installed, speed in those five locations immediately dropped 22% from 44mph to 34mph. Now, we see those signs everywhere.

We are on a constant lookout for information that provides us with direction on what actions we should take. Feedback Loops provide us with this direction by telling us how we are performing relative to a certain standard. In the study mentioned above, that standard was a speed limit. When we encounter a feedback loop, we automatically change our behavior to align with what we believe should be "better."

Implementing feedback loops into your CRM automations, membership programs, and in-store experience (if you have a brick-and-mortar location) will bring out the best levels of engagement in your customers. It could also very well lead to a boost in sales. Gamification technology is a great example of using feedback loops in all kinds of areas in business.

Limited Access[79]

Research shows that we attribute a significantly higher value to things when there are barriers in the way of getting access to them, as well as when there are barriers in the way of others getting access to what we already have. This effect is a more specific form of *Scarcity*.

The threat of scarcity and allure of exclusivity is what drives us to pursue limited-edition products and limited-access services. If you have a product that is able to be modified in a certain way to create this Limited Access effect, it may be in your interest to create it.

---

78 Public Office (2003). Speed radar feedback sign study. City of Garden Grove, California.
79 Ashley, Gillespie & Noble (2016). The effect of loyalty program fees on program perceptions and engagement. Journal of Business Research.

It is vitally important that your customers *pay* for that access. In a study of Amazon Prime members, those who paid for a subscription had a higher overall willingness to spend and had greater brand loyalty than Prime Members who were given a free trial.

Past Commitment Rationality[80]

In a study held in Iowa, over 200 homeowners opted to have their energy usage tracked for 12 months. The researchers in charge of the study told half of the group that their names would be published in the newspaper as a way of celebrating their commitment. After the study was over, the group that was told their names would be published had a 15.5% lower energy usage over the winter months.

In order to appear rational to others, we alter our behavior to match our past commitments, even when it is outside of our immediate priorities. This is called *Past Commitment Rationality.* When someone makes a commitment during a sales process, especially a conversation, they are affirming their future decision-making to work with you. Ensure that you receive these commitments early and often—and refer back to them if necessary.

Rewards[81]

When 58 homeowners in Philadelphia, PA were asked to have their grocery-buying habits monitored for 8 weeks, half were given a 50% discount reward on any fruit and vegetables they purchased, and the other half of the group was not.

After the study was over, it was found that the discount reward increased purchases of fruits and vegetables from 6.4 to 16.7 servings per household per week. The research indicates that the reward alone was the cause of this increase.

We are naturally motivated by rewards. Adding rewards to your customer journey, before and after the first purchase, will reliably increase the rate at which people engage with your marketing and ultimately buy from you. This is the foundation of the gamification frameworks that are making their way into digital marketing.

80　Pallak et al (1980). Commitment and energy conservation. Applied Social Psychology Annual, Volume 1, 235-253
81　Phipps et al. (2015). Impact of a rewards-based incentive program on promoting fruit and vegetable purchases. American Journal of Public Health, vol. 105

Semmelweis Reflex[82]

Ignaz Semmelweis was a Hungarian physician. In 1847, he discovered that 90% of childbed fever deaths could be prevented if doctors washed their hands in between seeing patients. Upon hearing this, his fellow doctors ridiculed him, in some cases rejecting the claim that a "gentleman's hands could transmit disease."

The *Semmelweis Reflex* is a reflex-like tendency to reject new evidence or new knowledge because it contradicts our established norms, beliefs, or paradigms.

A creative application of this NeuroTactic is the use of satire. By stating facts that are blatantly false or exaggerated, your audience will notice you more easily in their process of rejecting what you've said. Be careful not to abuse this effect. Remember—satire is a form of comedy. If you venture outside the realm of comedy in this case, you may put your brand reputation at risk.

Weber-Fechner Law[83]

"They" say if you want to boil a frog, put it in a pot of lukewarm water and slowly heat it on the stove. If you just throw the frog into boiling water, it will jump out. The human mind is similar to a frog in this respect. Our sensitivity to a task's complexity or duration diminishes over time. Given a slowly intensifying sequence of interactions with your brand, coupled with the right incentives and rewards, prospects will go to great lengths to engage with you.

Whether you are sending email broadcasts, running ads, making phone calls, or sending direct mail, your marketing is always "asking" for something from your prospects (even if it is time). By gradually increasing the intensity of your calls to action or points of commitment, you can generate higher levels of marketing engagement than if you would by asking for a heavy upfront commitment.

Zeigarnik Effect[84]

Pending assignments or tasks stay in our memory longer than completed assignments. When we try to remember all of our pending tasks, they come to

82 Mortell, Manfred; Balkhy, Hanan H.; Tannous, Elias B.; Jong, Mei Thiee (July 2013). "Physician 'defiance' towards hand hygiene compliance: Is there a theory–practice–ethics gap?". Journal of the Saudi Heart Association. 25 (3): 203–208.

83 Britannica, The Editors of Encyclopaedia. "Weber's Law." Encyclopædia Britannica, Encyclopædia Britannica, Inc., www.britannica.com/science/Webers-law.

84 Zeigarnik, B. (1938). On finished and unfinished tasks. A source book of Gestalt psychology, 1, 300-314

mind easily. If, on the other hand, we try to recall all of our completed tasks in the same time frame, we have more difficulty bringing them to mind. We feel a psychological weight of unfinished tasks, and have a higher recall rate of them, until they are completed.

Your customers are both consciously and unconsciously aware of the tasks they have left incomplete. In the case of your marketing and sales process, these incomplete tasks can range from reading an email to scheduling a sales call to signing a contract. Reminding your prospects and customers of these tasks, such as sending a cart abandonment email, will increase the likelihood that they will complete them. To get the most out of this effect, be sure to highlight the emotional release they will feel once the task is complete.

MEMORY

Our memories play an exceptionally large role in how we engage in daily life. We buy from brands we recognize, we laugh more easily at comedians we love, and we are more trusting of people we know. Memories form our opinions and worldview, and without them, we wouldn't be able to make the decisions that we do. That is why Memory is one of the most important categories of NeuroTactics. Use these principles wisely and they will set a strong foundation for your brand and customer loyalty for years to come.

Availability Heuristic[85]

When making decisions or judgments, we are more influenced by memories and thoughts that are easily recalled than those which are harder to remember. This is why documentaries have such an immediate effect on our beliefs toward the topic of the movie; our immediate thoughts are full of the arguments and reasoning we just saw in the documentary. Since we remember those arguments most clearly, they have more influence over our beliefs.

The Availability Heuristic can play to your favor or your demise. Since customers' opinions can be swayed in the short term through this method, it is important to know what competing marketing is out there influencing their opinions. Once you know that, you can take control of the narrative. Build your campaigns with an Educational style in a way that teaches the audience something they don't already know—but which supports your brand's position instead of that of your competitors.

---

85 Schwarz, Norbert; Bless, Herbert; Strack, Fritz; Klumpp, Gisela; Rittenauer-Schatka, Helga; Simons, Annette (1991). "Ease of retrieval as information: Another look at the availability heuristic". Journal of Personality and Social Psychology. 61 (2): 195–202.

Fluency Shortcut[86]

Mental fluency is similar to the thickness of a liquid. Short, easy-to-pronounce words are swallowed like water, whereas long, complicated words are swallowed like honey. Although honey still goes down, it takes more effort.

Our brains are built to treat more fluent words, ideas, images, and sounds with a higher priority than their less-fluent counterparts. In other words, our brains drink the water before they swallow the honey. As a result, we tend to remember short, punchy political slogans and we tend to forget long, complicated prayers and poems. With better memory of these "highly fluent" slogans comes a familiarity, a trust, and a willingness to spread.

To build fluency into your product, remove the friction associated with deciphering and remembering your core message. Simplify it as much as possible. When compared to a competing message, your customers will remember and believe the one that is easier to remember. Popular political slogans gain their virality through this single psychological principle.

Inaction Inertia Effect[87]

When we encounter a really great offer from a business, we have the choice to accept or reject it. Both of those decisions set a precedent in our minds which leads to a higher likelihood of making the same decision in the future with subsequent offers. In the case of rejection, however, the effect is stronger.

Black Friday is the biggest sales day of the season for retailers around the US. More often than not, consumers get access to the biggest discounts of the year on this single day. What retailers don't take into consideration, however, is that the overwhelm of Black Friday offers means customers *reject* more offers on this day than they normally would. When this happens, those same customers will have a *lower* likelihood of taking advantage of the same offer in the weeks and months to come. As we reject great offers, we become more resistant to offers for the same product, or even from the same brand, down the road.

Businesses who are offering discounts should consider the timing of their offers and the follow-up to customers who rejected those same offers. Change the offer entirely to sell a different line of products to the people who rejected an

---

86   Novemsky et al. (2003). Preference fluency and its effects on no-choice, compromise and attraction effects. Association for Consumer Research.

87   van Putten, M et al. (2013) How consumers deal with missed discounts: Transaction decoupling, action orientation and inaction inertia

offer in the past. And be careful not to inundate customers with special offers too often; it will cause them to de-value your products.

Mere Position Effect[88]

In a 2014 study of a hotel booking website, researchers found that the first and last items in the list of available hotels received the highest levels engagement out of all the options in the list. This is known as the Mere Position Effect.

Most readily applied to eCommerce websites, the Mere Position Effect gives marketers the opportunity to promote their highest-selling or most-profitable products by positioning them at the top and bottom of product galleries and lists.

Consider how you can use the Mere Position Effect on your own website, whether it is for a product range, a list of top-converting blog posts, or service information pages. If you are in a retail location, make use of this effect in menus, signage, and window prints.

Nostalgia Effect[89]

We are wired to place more value on products, places, and experiences that create a connection to the past. This is why vintage video game consoles and vinyl records still have a place in modern-day culture. Although their technology has been far surpassed, we still choose to pay a premium to get a slice of nostalgia from a product we once had.

Think about how you can incorporate nostalgic elements into your marketing or even your products. Carefully consider what "era" you want to help your customers return to (this will be based on their age demographic), and then do your research on what cultural references and visual styles you can use to create a "blast from the past."

Expression Bias

We all enjoy expressing our uniqueness to others, whether that is through our clothing, personality, or relationships. More to the point, we will pay a premium for the option of self-expression through the items and services we buy.

88   Ert & Fleischer (2016). Mere position effect in booking hotels online Journal of Travel Research, 55(3), 311-321.
89   Lasaleta, J.D., Sedikides, C. & Vohs, K.D. (2014). Nostalgia weakens the desire for money. Journal of Consumer Research, 41(3), 713-729

For example, placing a monogram on a shirt or electronic device makes it more "ours," and we attribute more value to it as a result.

People are always on the lookout for ways to communicate their identity to others. By providing a customization option, or product variants that reflect important characteristics of your customers' personalities, you will give them the capability of self-expression through your products or services. Coca Cola did this when they began printing peoples' names on their cans of soda, and Apple does this when they allow people to engrave their names on an iPhone.

Think about ways you can help your customers customize your products to their own liking. It may help them attribute more value to what they're buying.

Rhyme As Reason Effect[90]

If a phrase rhymes, we are more likely to believe it and remember it. Whether it is a political slogan or a company's tagline, rhyming words are easier for our brains to understand and remember, which makes them more familiar and easier to trust.

Think of ways to incorporate rhyming words into your campaign names, slogans, and headlines. This will increase the familiarity that someone feels when they encounter your marketing, ultimately leading to a higher sense of trust and willingness to engage with your brand.

Storyteller Bias[91]

We are more persuaded by, and remember more easily, people and companies that tell great stories. Our brains are hard-wired to remember stories more than any other type of information (especially numbers).

Your customers' perception of your brand is shaped by the stories you tell. By using a narrative to lead your branding and marketing efforts, you are using the most powerful form of communication to include your customers on an emotional journey.

Stories can be incorporated into every step of the customer journey, from advertising to phone calls. It is critical to investigate what the right stories are for your brand and to tell them in the right way. Stories can be short or long; the

---

90   McGlone & Tofighbaksh (2000). Birds of a feather flock conjointly: Rhyme as reason in aphorisms. Psychology Science.
91   Lundqvist et al (2013). The impact of storytelling on the consumer brand experience. The case of a firm-originated story. Journal of Brand Management.

choice depends on the channel through which you're communicating and the purpose of your story's existence in your campaign.

BEYOND THE MARKETING OPERATING SYSTEM

You are now ready to go off into the world and become your own Marketing Scientist. Congratulations! The skills you learned in this book, along with the marketing operating system you built along the way, are going to keep your marketing results sustainable and growing for years to come.

You've come a long way—and I mean that.

There aren't many people who go out of their way to learn the science of marketing, but you've stuck with it and come out the other side. And you are stronger for it. You now have the skills to evaluate every micro-niche offer that comes your way. You have the ability to interview candidates for marketing positions within your company. You can see your marketing operating system from a high level—from your Customers to your Campaigns to your Conversions—and understand how they are all connected.

Build A Culture Of Objectivity

The concepts shared in this book are based on a ruthless dedication to marketing science. With that comes a respect for data and numbers—but I know that not all companies are filled with people who have such an attitude of objectivity when it comes to marketing.

If this is the case in your business, then I would begin by having a few meetings with your team to present what you have found through conducting the exercises in this book on your own. Ask them how they would address fixing bottlenecks in your funnel. Ask them how to best address a failing marketing channel. After you have done this a few times, begin to present them with your own Customer Briefings, Campaign Briefings, and Split Test Briefings. Ask them for their candid feedback and be patient if they still don't catch on. I assure you, with time, they will start to come around and realize you are addressing serious priorities.

If you are in an urgent situation that requires a major turnaround, you will need to pull out the big guns. Odds are that your leadership team has called for one or more meetings to examine why your marketing isn't performing well. Before the next meeting is held, create three sets of briefings and bring them to the meeting. Print copies for as many people as are in the room. Email PDFs to those attending virtually. Grab the screenshare and the mic and walk through each document in detail to provide options for a plan to get out of the marketing "dumps." If you are not on the leadership team yet, I can guarantee this strategy is one of the fastest ways to get there.

Your company's culture of objectivity will define how successful your marketing operating system is. As with any implementation of a new system inside a business, you need buy-in from all levels of the organization. Be patient if you feel resistance. Be aggressive if you know it's an urgent matter. But most of all, don't give up on *using* this system, even if it is just for yourself at first. You will sleep better at night.

This book wouldn't exist without the support of my wife, family, clients, colleagues, and the talented teams at Vivid Labs and Morgan James Publishing. I will be forever grateful that you were all part of this journey.

ABOUT THE AUTHOR

Dan Russell is a speaker, author, entrepreneur, and marketing expert. Shortly after graduating from college, Dan built a seven-figure marketing agency that used scientific marketing principles to help client businesses grow. He now runs Vivid Labs, a marketing think tank dedicated to testing, publishing, and teaching cutting-edge marketing strategies to businesses around the world. He's also the writer at The Goldpan Report, a marketing trends newsletter for business owners and executives. Dan lives in Vero Beach, Florida with his wife Melanie.

GLOSSARY OF TERMS

Audience

This is a group of people who have a higher-than-average likelihood of buying your product. It can be broken down into your Minimum Viable Audience and your Secondary Audiences.

Big Idea Brainstorm

The BIG is a structured meeting dedicated to helping you come up with a Big Idea. It uses a series of creative marketing prompts to build new and interesting perspectives on your audience and your product.

Control

The control is the original version of the marketing asset, such as a landing page, that you are testing for improvements within a split test.

Conversion Rate

The conversion rate is the percentage of people that convert, or take a predetermined action. There are many types of conversion rates, from click-through rate to lead conversion rate. Conversion rates are calculated by dividing the total number of conversions over a given time period by the total number of people who had the opportunity to convert over the same time period. For example, a landing page conversion rate is calculated by dividing the number of leads by the number of people who visited the landing page.

Conversion Rate Optimization

This is the process of using the scientific method to plan and run experiments to increase the conversion rate of specific steps in your sales funnel.

CRM: Customer Relationship Management System

A CRM is an online platform that keeps track of your customer records. It has the capability to manage tags (ways of categorizing records), purchase history, marketing history, and other actions and notes that have been added to the customer over their experience with your brand. A CRM is essential for digital marketing purposes and should integrate with most, if not all, of your channels and sales funnel conversion steps. More often than not, a CRM will also have email marketing and merchant processing capabilities, among others.

Demographics

Ways of describing your audience with raw data such as age, gender, location, and income. Think about the data that a census collects—those are demographics. Another way to think of demographics is how your audience looks from the outside.

Funnel Conversion Rate

The percentage of people who complete the full funnel journey from the TOF (Top Of Funnel) to the BOF (Bottom Of Funnel). You can multiply your traffic levels by this number to predict how many sales you'll receive from current or future traffic levels. This number is also known as your Click-To-Sale Conversion Rate.

Key Performance Indicator (KPI)

A critical performance metric that is tracked over time. In the case of split testing, the KPI is the marketing performance metric your split test is designed to improve.

Landing Page

The landing page is the first page that someone will see after engaging with your marketing campaign's call to action. It contains a form that the visitor can fill out with their name and email address, and possibly more contact information that you will need for lead qualification purposes (like phone number or location).

Lead

A lead is considered to be a person who is interested in your product but not yet ready to buy. It's defined by having a new lead record in your CRM with at least one piece of contact information like an email address or phone number.

Marketing Campaign

A series of coordinated messages and pieces of content that have a common call to action and send members of your audience to the top of your sales funnel.

Minimum Viable Audience

The core audience that your marketing message should be aimed at. Your MVA contains the most fundamental targeting characteristics needed to reach a group of people that have a higher-than-average likelihood of buying from you.

Multivariate Testing

A process of advanced experimentation that uses more than one variable at a time during a testing period.

Neuromarketing

The combination of modern brain science and traditional direct-response marketing techniques. The NeuroTactics in this book are based within this discipline.

Psychographics

Methods of describing the behaviors and interests of your audience, such as buying habits, hobbies, and interests. This can be thought of as what your audience looks like from the "inside."

Secondary Audience

A smaller audience that has been "splintered" off from your Minimum Viable Audience in order to reach a smaller subset of your overall audience that shares a common characteristic.

Split Test (A/B Test)

These are well-planned marketing experiments designed to "try out" new forms of your copywriting, design, and customer experience in order to boost the performance of your sales funnel.

Tripwire Page

Tripwires are low-cost, low risk paid offers that you can make to a new lead. They are designed to lower the barrier to entry into your customer base, and they help convince a new lead to pull out their credit card and give your company a try. The first transaction is a critical moment in your customer journey, and it immediately increases the likelihood that they will purchase from you again.

Upsell Page

Also known as a One-Time Offer (OTO) page, an Upsell Page provides a one-time opportunity to add another product to the original tripwire product order. Since these pages are displayed immediately after a tripwire purchase, new customers' credit card information is often stored in the purchasing system so they can click one button to add the Upsell offer to their order without re-entering their payment information.

Variable

The variable is an important ingredient to a split test. It represents the element of your funnel that you want to change in order to reach an improvement in your marketing performance.

Variant

A variant (also known as a treatment) is a new version of the experiment's control that has had the variable changed in some way. For example, if you are testing the layout of a landing page, the current landing page (with no changes) is used as the experiment control while a duplicated version of the control, with a change in design, is used as the variant.

A free ebook edition is available with the purchase of this book.

To claim your free ebook edition:
1. Visit MorganJamesBOGO.com
2. Sign your name CLEARLY in the space
3. Complete the form and submit a photo of the entire copyright page
4. You or your friend can download the ebook to your preferred device

Morgan James
BOGO™

A **FREE** ebook edition is available for you or a friend with the purchase of this print book.

CLEARLY SIGN YOUR NAME ABOVE

Instructions to claim your free ebook edition:
1. Visit MorganJamesBOGO.com
2. Sign your name CLEARLY in the space above
3. Complete the form and submit a photo of this entire page
4. You or your friend can download the ebook to your preferred device

Print & Digital Together Forever.

Snap a photo   Free ebook   Read anywhere

CPSIA information can be obtained
at www.ICGtesting.com
Printed in the USA
JSHW031542190722
28162JS00001BA/2